Lasting Love

The Five Secrets of
Growing a Vital,
Conscious Relationship

Lasting
Love

Gay & Kathlyn Hendricks

RODALE

This edition first published in the UK in 2004 by
Rodale Ltd
7–10 Chandos Street
London W1G 9AD
www.rodale.co.uk

Printed and bound in the UK by CPI Bath using acid-free paper from
sustainable sources
1 3 5 7 9 8 6 4 2

A CIP record for this book is available from the British Library
ISBN 1–4050–6726–8

**This paperback edition distributed to the book trade by Pan
Macmillan Ltd**

149, 184
£13.00

WE **INSPIRE** AND **ENABLE** PEOPLE TO IMPROVE
THEIR LIVES AND THE WORLD AROUND THEM

To Polly and Bob Swift – wonderful parents, lasting lovers for fifty-plus years, and inspiration to everyone fortunate enough to know them.

Acknowledgments

We are deeply grateful to the several thousand partners who have entrusted us with facilitating their relationship journeys. They have taught what it means to be fully human. They are our heroes.

We have also been blessed to have many close friends and colleagues who have embraced our work and taken it into new dimensions. For their love, support, and inspiration during the past three decades we wish to thank Kate and Eddie, Katrin and Meinrad, Kenny and Julia, Jack and Inga, Annie and Douglas, Antje and Jochim, Lori and Chris, Geli and Bernd, Eva and Dieter, Jett and Marlena, Suzanne and Steve, Diana and Matt,

Grace and Michael, Barbara and Jim, Darsh and Susan, Ricardo and Monika, Bob and Roy, Christine and John, Nate and Corinna, Marcy and Paco.

Being supported by a great agent and editor is a rare, wonderful cause for celebration in a writer's life. Here, we were gifted lavishly by:

• The brilliant and subtle editorial touch of Jennifer Kushnier.

• The guidance of two women we feel very fortunate to know: Bonnie Solow, angel masquerading as agent, and Stephanie Tade, goddess disguised as editor.

Thank you, thank you, thank you all.

Contents

Introduction

Your New Path to Harmony and Vitality

A television crew came to do a feature on our work a while back. They followed us around for three days as we worked with couples, talked to each other over dinner, and so forth. The reporter did a great job with the interviews and on the ultimate televised feature as well. After the cameras were turned off, however, he let down his guard and got personal.

"You two are so upbeat and make it sound so doable, but is it really?" He said he'd seen plenty of *comfortable* couples, but he'd seldom met any who got closer *and* more creative as the years went by. He and his wife had struck a bargain—he would be the "star" and she would be the support person. Yet, the deal was already proving costly: She was depressed and he was restless. We could feel the despair he was carrying. Here he was—handsome, talented, young, articulate—and yet he had already given up and settled for less than what he envisioned his marriage could be.

We believe he speaks for millions of people. The evidence is dismal, both from personal observation and from the scientific research. If you look around your family, friendship network, and community, you probably cannot find very many people in long-term relationships who are thriving as creative individuals and growing closer as lovers at the same time. The norm in stable long-term relationships tends to be more in the direction of comfort, compromise, and, sometimes, truce.

Although we were growing up on opposite edges of the country, we both remember having a similar moment of insight when we were at school. For Kathlyn, the awareness came while watching her parents and their friends play a party game in a high state of alcohol-inspired merriment. She saw her parents laughing and talking animatedly, two things she never saw them do in normal life. She thought, "If this is as good as it gets for adults, I don't want anything to do with it." For Gay, the awareness came when he was asked to write an essay on something he believed in strongly. He chose the subject, "Why I will never get married." He said that he'd never seen a person who was both married and lively. The married couples he saw in his family and town all looked bored, pained, and trancelike, as if they were sleepwalking on a rocky road.

Through destiny or happy chance, we ended up turning these insights into productive careers rather than cynical bitterness. By holding out for what we really wanted, we also managed to get through the maze of fate to find each other. Ultimately, the guy who vowed never to get married found (and married!) the girl who decided never to grow up. We channeled our energies into discovering ways to become closer and more fully ourselves in the course of a long-term relationship. Now, after twenty-some years and several thousand couples sessions, we've finally put all the pieces of the program in place.

First and foremost, we are our own best customers, as any therapist or relationship expert must be. We did a great deal of research in the laboratory of our own hearts and minds in order to find out how to keep our own relationship growing bountifully. Even if we had never shared the tools in Lasting Love with other couples, we would know in our hearts that they work.

Lasting Love is our most comprehensive work, and at the same time our simplest. The program rests on the foundation of five solid principles and is brought to life with five radically simple techniques. We call them "radically" simple in the spirit of the original Latin word, *radix*, which means "root" or "core." Although simple, each of the central techniques changes the core dynamics of the relationship whenever it is applied.

THE FLOW OF LOVE

What is the most important thing in your life?

After giving it some thought, you'll probably agree with us that the most important thing in life is the feeling of love inside and around you. If you feel the flow of love in your life, you have a springboard to miracles under your feet with every step. If you don't feel the flow of love, you could be a billionaire and feel like a pauper. Without love, you could be a movie star and not be able to look at your face in the mirror.

We know this firsthand because several thousand couples have come through our office doors over the past twenty years. All of them were seeking to restore the flow of love between them. A few of them were billionaires and movie stars you'd recognize. All of them had problems you'd recognize. They are the same problems we've faced in our own marriage. They are the exact problems that you and everyone else will face in a committed relationship.

On the surface, the problems revolve around specific issues:

How can you end blame and criticism?

How can you stop arguing about money?

How can you keep passion and romance alive over time?

How can you agree on how to parent the kids?

Beneath those specific issues, though, are bigger questions that everyone must answer:

How can you thrive in a long-term relationship as a creative individual and as an intimate partner?

How can you use the inevitable challenges of a long-term relationship as a springboard to greater closeness and creative vitality?

How can you ignite passion and vitality—and keep it glowing forever?

These were the questions we had to answer in our own marriage, and they were the questions that inspired much of our work in the decade after *Conscious Loving* was published.

Since 1990, we have worked with many people in long-term relationships: two thousand couples in private sessions, groups, and seminars. These relationships ranged from seven to fifty-two years in length, with an average length of twelve years, were mostly heterosexual, and were racially and ethnically diverse. We were interested in discovering what saps the vitality from long-term relationships and what can make the vitality surge again. We were especially interested in finding out what people could do to prevent vitality from decreasing in the first place. Here is the essence of what we learned.

THE KEY DISCOVERY

In nine out of ten long-term relationships, vital energy slowly drains away because of problems in five specific areas. Even if the couple's surface conflict concerns sex or money, the real source of the problem is usually rooted in at least one of these five issues:

- Commitment

- Emotional transparency

- Sharing responsibility

- Creative individuation

- Appreciation

If you address these problems with five simple techniques, you can generate passion and harmony, even if those qualities have been absent for years.

Let's walk through a brief summary of the five insights that comprise the foundation of *Lasting Love*.

The First Insight

Every relationship conflict is rooted in a hidden commitment problem, even if the partners have been nominally committed for decades. If this commitment issue is addressed correctly, it becomes a catalyst for a profound breakthrough in harmony and creative energy.

Although most of the research on this commitment principle was carried out in marital relationships, we also confirmed it in the business world through our consulting work in approximately eighty companies. As we convey in lectures, this principle applies in the boardroom as well as in the bedroom. By analyzing hundreds of conflicts, we discovered that the problem often began with an unmade commitment. In other words, someone (or sometimes all parties) did not fully commit to a significant activity in the partnership. We worked out a simple way to find where the commitment problem was located and a technique for rapidly moving through the impasse, which we'll reveal in chapter 2.

The Second Insight

Relationships flourish in an atmosphere of emotional transparency, especially when both people speak clearly about their deeper emotions such as fear, sadness, and longing.

In the *Lasting Love* program, partners learn how to speak difficult truths in friendly ways. For example, if you speak bluntly to your partner—as in, "I'm gonna get you for flirting with Chris at the party"—you will invariably experience conflict. However, if you use our friendly technique of microscopic

truth—as in, "When I saw you talking to Chris I got scared"—
you will get a much friendlier response. The first communication contains a threat, "I'm gonna get you," and an arguable
perception, "flirting with Chris." Even if you could get everybody at the party to agree that your partner was flirting with
Chris, the statement would still trigger conflict.

The second communication contains a personal perception,
"When I saw you . . . ," and an unarguable feeling-statement, "I
got scared." Reliably, this move stops conflict and opens a space
for resolution. In fact, our research indicates that once either
partner speaks a sentence like this, a resolution usually occurs
within ten minutes.

Interestingly, a gender difference emerged from our research: Breakthroughs often occur when men speak plainly
about fear, sadness, and longing and when women speak plainly
about anger. We tailored different communication strategies to
the differing communication styles of men and women, and
we'll describe these strategies in detail in chapter 3.

The Third Insight

Relationships thrive only when partners share responsibility for
issues and duties. On a daily basis, vitality grows when each
person takes full responsibility for any issue that arises. Vitality
surges when both partners stop blaming and start claiming
ownership of problems.

By contrast, most people try to apportion responsibility by
asking the wrong question: Whose problem is it? This question
always leads to blame, conflict, and power struggles. For example, a conflict about money may recycle for years, but it will

get resolved only when each person claims full responsibility for the problem. When one person in a relationship habitually takes more than 100 percent responsibility for issues that arise, the other partner gets away with taking less than 100 percent responsibility. It is essential to correct this pattern so that balance can be attained in the relationship.

People squander massive amounts of creative energy in relationships when partners point the finger of blame at each other. With the Responsibility Principle, which we'll further discuss in chapter 4, partners meet on the equal ground of full ownership, thus eliminating the wasted energy of blame and power struggles.

The Fourth Insight

In nearly every long-term relationship, one partner consistently puts more energy into the relationship than the other partner. Over time, this imbalance causes the initiator to feel tired and unappreciated. The solution is *not* to focus on getting the other partner to change and put forth more energy, but for the initiator to make a commitment to his or her own creativity. In practical terms, the initiator must do something purely for self-expression (not for others) at least one hour per week.

Our research has found that it takes only one hour a week of creative self-expression (e.g., journaling, learning an instrument, dancing, going on nature walks, meditating) to produce more vital energy in the individual and thus in the relationship. Of course, more than one hour is preferable, and surprisingly, the other partner begins to shift in positive directions as the initiator devotes more time and energy to individual creative expression. We'll show you how to begin expressing your creativity in chapter 5.

The Fifth Insight

Relationship vitality starts to wane in an "appreciation gap," and vitality continues to drain away as this gap widens. We can help pinpoint a specific place and time where the break first occurred in the ongoing flow of appreciation. Specific techniques can then restore the flow of appreciation, and this flow liberates creative energy in the partnership.

Partners speak appreciatively to each other in the early stages of a relationship, and although the appreciations may vary from the insightful to the trite, at least they are frequent. For example, statements such as "I like the way you look tonight" and "You make me feel like the luckiest person in the world" are more likely to be spoken in the first year than in the tenth. As time passes, couples speak fewer appreciations, instead devoting more and more time to solving problems. Problem solving is often directed outwardly toward children, maintenance of house and property, and other items that need constant attention. Usually, partners direct problem solving toward themselves only when conflict occurs.

One of our clients told us, "I knew my marriage was over the day I got off an airplane, expecting a welcoming hug and kiss, and instead was greeted with, 'The upstairs toilet broke again.'" Fortunately, this couple was able to achieve Lasting Love again by balancing their problem solving with more spoken appreciations. We'll guide you through appreciations in chapter 6.

TIME FOR A NEW PARADIGM

In long-term relationships, most of us proceed slowly through a period of learning-love before we reap the harvest of genuine love. In learning-love, the unconscious goal is to get something in return for your love. You want to get approval, for example, or get confirmation that you are loveable. Genuine love is not about *getting*, nor is it about completing yourself in any way. Genuine love is between two people who know they are already complete. Genuine love is based on a new paradigm in which both partners are committed to the celebration of each other and their loved ones.

If partners in a relationship are willing to practice the simple techniques in *Lasting Love*, they will get an immediate payoff in the form of a quantum shift in the level of harmony and creative energy, both in themselves and in the relationship. The heart and soul of the new paradigm is the celebration of essence. Essence is the word we use for the unconditioned, authentic self, the person we truly are beneath all the learned survival responses of early life. The higher purpose of love relationships is to bring essence to light, revealing the essential creative self beneath all the personas everyone uses to survive and get recognition. In order for relationships to flourish, the essence of each person must be recognized and brought forth. If we are not willing to reveal who we truly are—or if we are not willing for our partners to reveal their true selves to us—conflicts will always follow in the aftermath of this decision to stonewall essence.

The new paradigm comes with a comprehensive set of communication tools. *Lasting Love* is a program that employs these tools that anyone can use to transform relationships at home and at work. Useful with both adults and children, these new activities produce magical results in relationships, even if only one person applies them. When both people in a relationship understand the principles and practice the activities, however, they achieve a substantial enhancement of closeness and creative energy.

YOUR ACTION PLAN

At the end of each chapter you will find your Action Plan. The Action Plan consists of three elements:

• Your Commitment

• Your Ongoing Practice

• Your Ten-Second Technique

The commitment is the agreement with yourself and your partner to apply the wisdom in the chapter you've just read. For example, as you'll see in chapter 2, you'll begin to apply the material on commitment by making the following agreement: "I commit to learning from all my interactions and from the results of my actions."

Your Ongoing Practice is the way you'll go about applying the material from day to day. Your Ten-Second Technique is the simplest, most effective technique for applying the wisdom of the chapter. You're welcome to invent other techniques, of course, but you'll find that the Ten-Second Technique will always work when others fail. It's been tested and refined with thousands of people; you can count on it.

149, 184

A NEW WORLD IS POSSIBLE

We want to live in a world where all of us can feel the warm embrace of genuine intimacy instead of settling for the numbing couch comforts of compromise. We want to live in a world where each of us also gets the chance to contact and express our full creative potential.

We bet you want to live in that kind of world, too.

From working on ourselves and with our clients, we know that this new world is possible. We also know that it is earned, not inherited or given. It is created by ordinary people with the will and courage to make extraordinary commitments. It is done one step at a time, with persistence and a good map.

Lasting Love is that map. It was created "the hard way," by many trials and many errors. We tell our students: If we know anything at all about relationships, it's because we've made every mistake ourselves at least once and worked with it in others at least a dozen times. For us, the road was not always easy, but the rewards are beyond anything we ever imagined. If our map can save people from taking unnecessary detours and hitting speed bumps at a jarring pace, we will feel doubly rewarded.

If it assists you in feeling the incredible vitality we've reveled in over the past two-plus decades, we will feel that our life purpose has been fulfilled.

Lasting Love

CHAPTER 1

Five Secrets of Lasting Love

ere's the bottom-line truth we discovered from our decades of work with couples in long-term relationships: People can *endure* long-term relationships in many ways, but they will only *thrive* if they do five things. In other words, you can grow older with your partner in many ways, but you will only grow closer and more creative through the steady practice of five actions.

We believe these five actions should be taught in every classroom in every school, every day. They most definitely should not be secrets we have to seek or stumble onto by trial and error. Yet they are. Almost none of us begin our love relationships knowing how to do these simple things, and our relationships are disastrous as a consequence.

Let's permanently remove the veil that has covered these secrets and begin a new era of intimacy in close relationships.

THE FIRST SECRET

If you want a close, vibrant love relationship, you need to become a master of commitment.

We teach couples how to make real commitments to each other. There is an art to commitment, but almost nobody knows how to practice it. The first step of this art is to spot and acknowledge the unconscious commitments that cause us to sabotage the harmony of our close relationships. For example, suppose a politician were to be caught having an adulterous relationship. Imagine how it would change that person's life, as well as the lives of the constituents, if the politician identified and acknowledged his unconscious commitments by saying, "From the evidence, I'm slowly beginning to realize that I'm committed to philandering, sexual betrayal, and lying. I also appear to be committed to getting caught. I'm committed to finding out if people will still like me after they find out I'm a bad boy." In practical reality, the act of claiming ownership of an unconscious commitment changes a troublesome dynamic in a relationship faster than anything else.

The second step of the art of commitment is to make commitments you can stand by. Real commitments can be made only about things you have control over. Real commitments are verifiable. If you make a phony commitment—such as, "I promise to love you forever"—you set up an impossible situation by promising an illusion. Nobody can commit to loving someone forever because some days you won't even wake up feeling loving toward yourself. Love is a mystery—part feeling, part spirit, part mind—and mysteries by their very nature are outside our control. A real commitment would be to commit to telling your partner the truth about when you're feeling loving and when you're not. This type of commitment saves relationships while turning on the flow of intimacy and creativity.

The *Lasting Love* program offers a specific set of commitments we've thoroughly tested with many couples. When couples make these commitments, their relationships thrive.

THE SECOND SECRET

If you want a long-term relationship that's both close and creatively vital, you have to become emotionally transparent. To go all the way to ultimate closeness and full creative expression, you must eliminate all barriers to speaking and hearing the truth about everything.

We teach couples how to listen to the truth about everything from their partners, and we teach them how to speak the truth about everything to their partners. Everything means everything: feelings, deeds, hopes, dreams. We ask them to consider any hesitation about telling or hearing the unvarnished truth to be a symptom of resistance to greater love and creativity.

We know this move is radical because it produces huge bursts of creative energy in everyone who tries it. As a practice, it has awesome power. As a concept, it quickly polarizes people—we've seen talk show audiences erupt in cheers and boos when we've said couples need to tell the truth to each other about everything. After twenty-plus years, though, we've still found no exceptions to the truth rule.

THE THIRD SECRET

If you want a long-term relationship that's both close and creatively vital, you must break the cycle of blame and criticism— it's an addiction that saps creative energy as surely as drugs or drink.

We invite couples to turn their relationships into blame-free zones. We teach each partner to take full responsibility for everything that occurs in the relationship, especially if it looks like it's the other person's fault. Radical responsibility—and the powerful creative energy it unleashes—comes from catching yourself in the midst of saying, "Why did you do that to me again?" and shifting to, "What am I doing that keeps inviting that behavior?"

We ask couples to go on a strict no-blame diet and stick to it. As a practice, this move liberates tremendous energy. In fact, we've seen life-altering breakthroughs come about when couples simply went one full day without criticizing or blaming each other. As a concept, the idea of giving up blame and criticism is often greeted with derision. "Impossible," some say. "How boring," say others. We have found that it's actually possible and anything but boring. The couple who is deeply addicted to blame and criticism has usually come to mistake the adrenalized drama of conflict for the flow of connection. The idea of life without the adrenalin may seem dull and empty at first, much like a lifelong flagellant must feel that first day without the self-administered whip.

THE FOURTH SECRET

If you want a vibrant long-term relationship—one in which you feel close as a couple and creative as individuals—you have to do something radical about your creativity. You have to take your attention away from fixing the other person and put it on expressing your own creativity. Even one hour a week of focusing on your own creativity will produce results. More than that will often produce miracles.

Nothing will sap your vital energy faster than squelching your creativity. Often, couples stifle their individual creativity in order to focus on fixing and changing the other person. Since this seldom produces tangible results, they devote more energy to the other person as a fixer-upper and less to individual creativity. When results are not forthcoming, they complain about the other person to third parties. They enter a dangerous cycle of complaint that has addictive properties—the more you do it the more things there are to complain about. Ultimately this leads to dissipation of creative energy and inner despair.

By contrast, fully creative people don't have time for complaint. Even if you're not fully engaged in creativity (even, as our research indicates, if you're doing only an hour a week of creative expression), you will see quantum enhancement of vitality within the relationship with every increase in creative self-expression.

THE FIFTH SECRET

If you want to create vital, long-lasting love, you must become a master of verbal and nonverbal appreciation.

We teach couples how to appreciate each other spontaneously and frequently. Although this may sound like a simple thing, it most definitely is not. In fact, it's the last thing we teach in the program because it's the hardest to learn. To utter a clear, heartfelt appreciation to another person is radical partly because it's so rare. To receive such an appreciation from another person is equally challenging. Most of us have never seen or heard a rich flow of spoken appreciations in relationships. In fact, many people cannot recall a single instance of clear appreciation in their families of origin.

The simple solution is to speak a heartfelt ten-second appreciation to the other person, *for no reasons other than to signify a commitment to appreciation and to open the flow of appreciation.* In other words, the spoken appreciation is not to get a particular result from the other person. In reality, it produces powerful results very quickly, but it is important that the appreciation not be spoken as a manipulation or in expectation of a reward.

We teach couples how to say simple and complex appreciations, ranging from "I like the way you did your hair today" to "Throughout our lives together, I have been repeatedly amazed by how generous you are." Although most couples can learn the art in an hour, they tell us that it takes the better part of a year's daily practice to savor its full value.

These five secrets have a revolutionary effect on any relationship in which they're practiced. The five secrets move people quickly through the stuck places so that they can enjoy the profound beauty of genuine love. We will have a great deal more to show you about these five secrets when we explore them in the chapters to come. First, though, let's go a little deeper into what we mean by genuine love.

DIFFERENT LOVES

Before defining genuine love, let's make a distinction between toxic attraction and love of any kind. In toxic attraction, people who fundamentally don't like or respect themselves invite others like them into their lives. They form entanglements in order to have company in their misery. They want fellow victims to complain to and to complain about. They want others to join them in their path of self-destruction. Based on our experience in relationship counseling, we've seen that toxic attraction is the foundation for about 5 percent of relationships. Fortunately that's only about one out of twenty relationships, but the statistics mean nothing if you are the one out of those twenty.

Now let's make a further distinction. In most long-term relationships, love grows through two stages: learning-love and genuine love. Most of us proceed slowly through a period of learning-love before we reap the harvest of genuine love. Learning-love is about learning those things you need to learn in order to feel genuine love. Learning-love is about repeating lessons until you get them. In learning-love, you pull certain people into your life to learn something only they can teach you. Once you learn that lesson, you enter a deeper relationship with that person or move on to another. The quest is for genuine love, and learning-love is a step along the way.

In learning-love, you are trying to get something: the love you think you need, approval, repeated reminders to be in touch with your feelings, reminders to stand up for yourself. Genuine love, however, is not about *getting* anything. It's about living in a flow of giving and receiving. In learning-love, you struggle over control of space and time: You crave more space or more closeness, or you think your partner is too slow or too fast, too full of feelings or too shut off from them. There is either too much or not enough sex, money, intimacy.

Learning-love is between two people who do not feel whole; each person feels lacking in something. They throw themselves into love in order to learn, and when they have learned to feel whole—when they have discovered that there is no lack that can be filled from outside them—then they may embark upon the journey of genuine love. Genuine love, on the other hand, is not about completing yourself. Genuine love is between two equals who know they are complete in themselves.

We know all of this firsthand because we've been there and back. Both of us have had many lessons in the painful school of learning-love. We've signed up for courses with names you'll probably recognize:

"Trying to save another person from his/her self-destructive tendencies."

"Trying to critique and improve the other person while overlooking major flaws of our own."

"Trying to get love and approval from someone who is stingy with both."

Genuine love is a new paradigm—not about survival, not about getting. It's based on a commitment both to celebration and to making a space in which others can celebrate.

The lesson of learning-love is simple but maddeningly hard to master. It is this: *You* are the creator of your life. If you desire more intimacy than the tiny amount you're getting, it's because you—for some conscious or unconscious reason—have made up the rule that you can have only a tiny amount of intimacy. If you don't feel you have the space you need to grow, it's because you—for some conscious or unconscious reason—have made up the rule that you can't have space to grow.

It takes most of us many years to master the lesson of learning-love. In fact, we've seen many intelligent people go to their graves without seeming to experience any genuine love. If it doesn't take you that long, lucky you! It took us many years of work before we went to bed and woke up every day experiencing genuine love. It's an idea with so much power that it scares a lot of people away. The couch comforts of victimhood offer a much safer place from which to watch life. Of course, the problem with that kind of safety is that you don't get to participate fully in life and love. You miss out on the exhilarating satisfactions of accessing your deep potential and contributing to others.

Needless to say, we're big advocates for going all the way to realizing your full potential. We don't encourage anyone to settle for "okay" when magnificence is freely available.

FOCUS ON COMMITTING, CREATING, AND APPRECIATING

In order for an intimate relationship to survive past the first few years, couples often get some trial-and-error skills in speaking the truth and taking responsibility. If they don't, the relationship usually falls apart around those two issues. The average length of a romantic relationship has decreased over the years, and at present seems to be in the range of four to four and a half years. We find that when couples in long-term relationships come to us, they have stumbled their way to some understanding of the importance of truth and responsibility in their relationship. Commitment, creativity, and appreciation, however, are a different matter. Oddly enough, almost no one begins with a conceptual grasp of or a practical fluency in these arts.

There's no reason any of us should be good at them whatsoever. After all, most of us receive no training, formal or informal, in how to make genuine commitments, how to access lifelong creativity, or how to deliver meaningful appreciations. As therapists and seminar leaders, we have witnessed hundreds of occasions when a single act of appreciation—expressed simply and from the heart—brought people closer together in a heartbeat's time. We have also witnessed the near miraculous power that a shift in commitment produces by opening the gateway to intimacy. We have seen people change (and sometimes save) their lives by expressing their creativity.

Discovering the secrets to commitment, creativity, and appreciation has been the most exciting professional and personal journey of our lives thus far. We are tremendously enthusiastic about sharing the secrets of these arts. This set of skills will equip anyone with a powerful and reliable method for enhancing the flow of connection in any relationship. Although we will focus mainly on love relationships, these skills also apply to business, friendship, parenting, and other areas where the flow of connection is paramount.

ACTIVE SKILLS

Many people wrongly think that commitment, creativity, and appreciation are passive states of being. They incorrectly assume that you're either committed or you're not, you're creative or you're not, you're appreciative or you're not. The good news is quite the opposite: These are active arts—skills you can practice from moment to moment.

Putting Commitment into Action

Let us show you what we mean with a brief story about the power of the new paradigm.

WE WERE SITTING with a man and a woman in our office, trying to help them out of a marital jam so long in the making and so long overlooked that it felt like death hovered in the room with us. They'd been together fourteen years, and it had essentially been fourteen years of struggle. After hearing their story, we asked them to do something radical: We asked them to declare this marriage dead. "If you will declare this marriage dead, we will ask you a question that will bring a new one to life or help you walk away from the death of this one with fewer wounds."

They were puzzled, but they went along with us and declared it dead.

We paused for a full minute of silence to honor the death of a noble effort that turned awful. When our minute was up, all of us opened our eyes. We asked them:

"What did you learn from this marriage that you could not have learned any other way?"

The question caught them by surprise, and they answered it candidly.

In the years since we first asked that question, we've heard people speak their replies in hundreds of different ways. No matter how they word it, people often come down to saying the same two things:

1. **"I found out the hard way that I'm more committed to my old patterns than I am to loving and being loved."**

In other words, they gradually put a commitment to an old pattern (criticizing, overdrinking, controlling) ahead of the commitment to the relationship. They didn't know how to make a conscious commitment to the relationship that was bigger than their unconscious commitment to their respective destructive patterns.

2. **"I discovered too late that I didn't get or give enough appreciation, and I waited until too late to do anything about it."**

In other words, they were unskilled and stingy in the area of appreciation.

Next, we asked them another question:

"Given the demise of this marriage, and given what you've learned from it, are you willing to make a commitment to a new marriage? Are you willing to create a marriage in which you both feel fully appreciated and you make the relationship more important than your old patterns?"

We asked them to consider the question carefully, in the quiet of their own minds and hearts, and then give us a clear yes or no.

After thirty seconds or so of silence, they spontaneously opened their eyes at the same time. They both nodded and said, "Yes."

The air cleared. The energy in the room lightened as their faces relaxed. We all sat back in our chairs, knowing there was work to be done but also knowing there was a new possibility that had not existed before.

Next, we asked: "Would each of you be willing to devote the same amount of energy to expressing your creativity that you've been using to fuel your conflict?"

Again, they were caught by surprise. It hadn't occurred to them that the exact same energy that's required to drive conflict could be used to inspire and express creativity.

Eventually they agreed to turn their conflict energy into creative energy, but they were quick to tell us they didn't know how.

"Nobody does," we said, "but once you make the commitment, the exact path always reveals itself."

The miracle unfolded over the next two months and continues to blossom now. They made good on their initial "yes," using the new techniques of commitment and appreciation that we describe later in the book. Within two months they had created something brand new, and during a four-year-later follow-up session, they said it was unimaginably better than their "first" marriage. In fact, they said that because they hadn't understood commitment and appreciation, the first marriage had been doomed from the beginning. Even though their first marriage had lasted fourteen years and this new one only four years so far, it felt as if the first one never existed.

That's the power of commitment, the first principle of the new paradigm. Now, take a closer look at appreciation.

Alternating Cycles

Human beings alternate between two ongoing cycles: a cycle of complaint or a cycle of appreciation. The ratio between the two—the amount of time we spend in each—determines how happy we are and how much happiness we inspire around us. It also affects how much creativity we express and inspire in others.

The cycle of complaint goes as follows:

We want or need something from our partner, such as more communication, more understanding, more touch, more freedom. For some reason, however, often lost in the mists of childhood, we're unconsciously committed to *not* getting those things. Inevitably our partner fails to give us what we want, so we complain about it and criticize our partner for his or her faults and failures.

The situation usually doesn't improve (or if it does, it improves only temporarily before returning to baseline or worse). We complain and criticize more, which leads to greater awareness of our partner's insufficiencies. Armed with more detailed evidence, we escalate our barrage of criticism and complaint.

We've worked with couples who had been recycling the same complaint for decades. Our conclusion—which surprised us at first—is that nobody ever gets better by being criticized. Almost everybody who criticizes, though, is convinced that if they keep it up long enough it will have the proper motivational effect on the other person.

Let's look at a better way. The cycle of appreciation goes as follows: We look for things to appreciate about our partners. We discover new ones or notice old ones anew. We speak our appreciations clearly. We see more things to appreciate, which leads to a greater awareness of our partner's value.

Living in a cycle of complaint consumes the very energy needed for creative expression. Living in a cycle of appreciation frees up energy that each person can use for individual and mutual creativity.

Appreciation in Action

What most of us need to know is this: We have a choice about which cycle to live in. What most of us *really* need to know is this: how to shift quickly out of the cycle of complaint and into the cycle of appreciation.

We've been running a large-scale research survey, via our Web site, on the subject of appreciation. One of our research associates sent Gay a note a while back in which she articulated her own reaction to something that happened at a dinner with us. Here's what she wrote:

"SPEAKING OF APPRECIATION, I remember the first time I ever saw a clear example of it. The three of us were in a restaurant together when we first met. At one point in the conversation Kathlyn said something funny. I vividly remember you turning to her and saying, out loud, casually, as if it was the most natural thing in the world: "One of the things I really love and appreciate about you is your fantastic sense of humor. You make my life so much richer because of how you look at the world. I was just feeling grateful for that and wanted you to know it." Kathlyn smiled warmly and thanked you, and then you both returned to our previous conversation.

I sat there perplexed for a moment. Although I'd seen strong, stable marriages before, I'd never seen this kind of communication. It's not the way most people talk, nor is it really the way most people think, either. Later, I realized that I was waiting for the punch line. I expected you to follow your appreciation with something teasing or funny or even insulting, and when it didn't come, I didn't know quite what to think. My mind was thinking: "Wait a minute . . . so you're just going to appreciate her? Out of the blue? For no reason? Without wanting any-

thing in return?" I think I learned something brand new about relation-
ships that day.

Embedded in her observation are important insights into a
new paradigm of relationships. For example, it surprised her to
see one of us appreciate the other "out of the blue" and "for no
reason." In other words, she witnessed appreciation for its own
sake, with no other agenda running as a subtext of the communication. In addition, the appreciation was spoken "without
wanting anything in return." In other words, it was not designed
to produce an outcome or result. This latter observation distin-
guishes the art of appreciating from the related art of praising.
There is no question that praise is a useful and important skill—
many books are available on how to do it effectively. For example, in the classic book, *The One-Minute Manager*, authors Ken
Blanchard and Spencer Johnson show how to use praise to reward good performance and shape employees' behavior in a positive direction. In Thomas Gordon's books on parent
effectiveness and teacher effectiveness, he presents a method-
ology for influencing children's behavior by the power of praise.

That's *not* what we're talking about.

The art of appreciating operates in a different paradigm,
which may be why there aren't many books about how to do it.
As we will show later, the paradigm in which appreciation occurs is not linear, nor is it intended to produce a specific result.
It does not fit within a reward-and-punishment schema. You
shift into the new paradigm by making a conscious decision, a
commitment to base your relationships on an ongoing flow of
positive energy—of genuine love. You choose to focus on appreciation "for its own sake," not to influence the behavior of

the other person. In spite of this, or perhaps because of it, the skills of Active-Appreciating and Conscious-Committing actually have a profoundly positive effect on other people's behavior. Things change for the better the moment either of these skills enters a relationship.

Here is an example of appreciation for its own sake, drawn from our own relationship:

GAY: One morning I awoke early to do some writing. After an hour or so I took a break to meditate, and during meditation an idea popped into my mind. I wrote thank you! about a dozen times with different-colored ink, and then cut the paper into strips with a pair of scissors. Each strip had a "Thank you!" on it. I put a "Thank you!" on each step of the stairs Kathlyn would take after she woke up. I was upstairs when I heard her sleepy footsteps approach the steps. Suddenly I heard a giggle, and then another and another as she came up the stairs and encountered each of my thank yous. When she came down she was absolutely aglow.

Can you think of a better way to start the day? (If so, please let us know so we can try it.)

A NEW PARADIGM OF
RELATIONSHIPS

We believe that concepts such as Conscious-Committing and Active-Appreciating constitute a shift in context that fundamentally alters the way in which people regard intimate relationships. This new paradigm is what caught our research associate's attention that night.

Prior Contexts

Up until very recently, the context of intimate relationships was clouded by survival fears. Although survival is not the main priority for millions of people when they wake up each day, it still is for many others. Fears about hunger, deprivation, and other survival issues still shape the nature of many relationships. For example, survival fears make it important to do one's duty by steadfastly inhabiting the roles prescribed by the prevalent social and religious authority structure. In times past, our ancestors paid less attention to psychological or spiritual fulfillment. Techniques for problem solving were essentially nonexistent.

Gay shares an illustrative story: "When I was at university, I mentioned to my grandfather that I was in therapy to 'handle some issues about my self-esteem.' He asked me what therapy was and chuckled as I explained it to him. I asked him how they handled such issues when he was a young man. 'Issues, hell,' he said. 'We were too busy handling plows.' He had run away from home at sixteen to avoid getting trapped in the role of a farmer. As long as he didn't have to handle a plow, he figured he'd handled the biggest issue he'd ever have to face. He and my grandmother had carved a home out of the Florida swamps, where they contended with snakes, alligators, and malaria on a regular basis."

Things changed as the twentieth century gained momentum. From our parents' time up until the present, the context of a relationship shifted toward "luxury items" such as the fulfillment of potential. Movies, literature, and other arts began to celebrate the transcendent possibilities of relationships—symbolized by the graceful dancing of Fred Astaire and Ginger Rogers. The Freudian revolution promised to offer tools for handling problems when missteps caused us to tread on each other painfully.

The New Context

It's a big shift from survival (handling plows) to fulfillment (handling issues). In the survival context, life is lived in waves with things like fear and hunger as the crests and periods of relief from those things as the swells. In the fulfillment context, life is lived in waves of fulfillment and the hunger for more. We believe, however, that the context is about to make an even larger shift, opening access to a new force field. This new force is electric with previously hidden potential. We believe that relationships in the new millennium will shift toward a focus on appreciation and celebration. The focus will be on the flow of connection.

The couples who come to us now want more than traditional problem-solving skills. As people become more sensitive to the flow of energy inside themselves and in their relationships, they are looking beyond traditional therapeutic techniques. They want life-skills they can use to awaken and enhance the flow of connection. The arts of committing and appreciating are the best ways we've found to deepen the flow of connection. A single act of skillful committing or appreciating instantly shifts the relationship into a more intensely experienced sense of flow and, thereby, creativity.

To imagine the kind of context shift we're talking about, think of a magician's tablecloth trick. Picture a fabulously set table with crystal glasses, bone china, and your heirloom silver. Imagine you and your beloved sitting down to dine amidst the beauty of the place settings, when suddenly you realize the tablecloth is made of . . . wax paper.

Quickly, though, you make a decision to enhance the quality of your life rather than despair over it. You snap your fingers and a magician appears. With a wink and a smooth flourish, the magician whips the wax paper out from under the place settings without disturbing them. With another magical move, he slides a crisp linen tablecloth under the place settings, without so much as rattling a teacup. Suddenly the essential beauty of what was there before is enhanced. Only one thing has changed, but it has changed everything.

That's not only a context shift; it's a conscious marriage of the power of your intention with your ability to create real magic.

That's the domain of the new paradigm.

PRACTICALLY SPEAKING

It takes only a split second to make a commitment to enhance your relationships. The moment changes everything, though, because you shift out of earlier contexts, such as survival and the search for fulfillment, into a new zone, full of new possibilities and based entirely on new questions.

In the survival context, relationships exist inside the question, "What must we do to survive?" Considerable time is spent shoring up defenses against hostile forces and carrying out chores in the rut of routine. There is little time or energy to search for fulfillment. You are watching and listening for threats to your survival.

In the fulfillment context, we live inside different questions, such as "What must we do to fulfill our potential?" and "How can we solve the problems that are the barriers to expressing that potential?" Considerable attention is paid to the past, where the barriers are presumed to have been erected. Considerable energy is consumed in power struggles about which partner bears responsibility for the barrier. You are watching and listening for clues on how to meet the needs of others and whether your own needs are being met.

In the new paradigm we offer in this book, the questions are profoundly different than survival or fulfillment. Your relationships live within questions such as:

- "What commitments do I need to embrace that will allow the relationship to flourish?"

- "What do I really admire and love about my partner?"

- "How can I best appreciate those qualities and actions?"

- "What can I do to make myself more available for appreciation?"

Although you have good problem-solving techniques at your disposal, you do not focus as much on problems. Instead, you look for what's right in the other person and in the relationship. You embark on a shared quest to find each other's essential qualities so that they may be skillfully appreciated.

You initiate your entry into the new paradigm with a conscious choice. Imagine life as a waiter or waitress, offering you a menu with three choices on it:

• Living your life in waves of fear

• Living your life in waves of fulfillment

• Living your life in waves of celebration

If you were going to pick one, what would your choice be?

In our relationship seminars, 99 percent of the participants choose celebration. There seem to be one or two people in every group who cannot imagine life without fear or the quest for fulfillment. Almost everyone else, though, sees that the conscious choice to organize your life around a context of appreciation opens up the greatest number of possibilities. If your life is about appreciation, you can celebrate even the days when your body is occupied by fear or your mind is preoccupied with a potential you haven't yet fulfilled.

CONTRASTING THE
OLD PARADIGMS WITH THE NEW

At dinner that evening, our research associate witnessed a communication that was not colored by survival or fulfillment. It came from the new paradigm, one in which there are no expectations embedded in the communications between partners. If you listen closely to the communications of most couples, you will see that some of their utterances may be colored by survival concerns, but a majority of them are surrounded by an aura of fulfillment and the lack thereof. Specifically, communications come with expectations embedded within them—or disappointment and anger that those expectations have not been fulfilled. Nowadays, when one partner says to another, "You forgot to get the potatoes at the store," he or she is not likely to be talking about a survival issue. The subtext of the communication might be, "How could you have forgotten to do something so simple?" or "If you loved me, you would have remembered the potatoes." She or he may be saying, "I don't feel loved and appreciated, and here's further evidence that I have every right to feel that way."

These patterns have a way of hardening into place with time so that within a few years most couples have developed rigid, predictable styles of communicating. One of our poet friends came by to visit us after being at a party with many long-married couples. She lamented that most of the couples looked like "matched pairs of glazed pots." That's the effect of staying too long in an old paradigm.

The new paradigm melts the glaze. The new paradigm gives an opportunity to break out of old forms into something new and vibrantly alive. But it doesn't stop there. The new paradigm extends from partner interactions to the larger arena of life as a whole. In its broadest application, the new paradigm is about how to live your whole life from a stance of gratitude rather than a stance of scarcity. It's about greeting each moment of life with an open heart rather than a judgmental mind. It asks you to express appreciation for no other reason than your decision to live a grateful life. Rather than waiting for life to bring experiences to you so that you can judge them worthy of appreciation, you initiate the new paradigm by taking a proactive stance of gratitude toward your life experience. You walk through life as a philanthropist instead of a supplicant, a producer instead of a consumer.

You become the generator instead of a battery. You provide your own energy instead of drawing on the energy of others. The difference is profound and comes with a magnificent surprise. The moment you choose to live life as a producer rather than a consumer of energy, you draw other people into your life who have chosen to live their lives as producers. The relationships you form with them magnify the energy of everyone, and you get more juice than you could ever have possibly imagined.

CHAPTER 2

The First Secret

*A New Kind of Commitment Gets
You Started*

WE'VE been together now for more than twenty rich and glorious years, but in the first year of our relationship we muddled around in circles. We recycled the same arguments, blamed each other for the same things, and then got up and did it all over again the next day. Then we discovered how commitment works, and everything changed. Now it's been years since we've had even the slightest argument. Instead of frittering away our energy in hassles, we use our passion to make love, write books together, go on long walks and bike rides, enjoy the rich friendships we've been blessed with.

You can do all that, and more, if you learn how commitment actually works.

All the major problems in relationships—money, sex, criticism, disagreements about how to raise kids—are rooted in hidden commitment problems. Fix the underlying commitment problem and the other problems will fix themselves. If you are having a problem in a relationship, it is very likely that you can fix it quickest by going to the source, and commitment is usually the source. In short, understand how commitment really works and your relationships will work wonderfully.

THE SECRET OF COMMITMENT

Essence is the word we use to describe the most precious part of ourselves. Your essence is who you really are at your soul's depths. Essence is the part of you that lets you know you're you. When you tune in deep inside, you recognize yourself by the presence of your essence. One of the high purposes of an intimate relationship is to create a space in which the essence of both people can grow to full flower.

Here's where commitment enters the picture: Essence can only be revealed in an atmosphere of true commitment. It is rare in relationships for partners to feel the growth of their own essence every day and to see the growth of essence in their partners. The reason it's so rare is that few of us understand how true commitment works. The moment we understand it, the light of essence dawns and the flow of deep connection begins.

True commitment begins only when we *pick one*. The art and science of commitment is knowing which person to pick and how to make a whole-being commitment to that person. The sad fact is that few of us get any training or education in how to make the kinds of commitments that allow relationships to work well. Advertising leads us to believe that it's picking the ring that makes a difference. That's ridiculous, of course, but most couples spend more time on that than they do on learning about the art and science of commitment.

First, ask yourself: Have you ever been given one second's training (much less one hour's or one day's) in the art of commitment? If not, join the club—we never received any, either.

Listen closely while we give you the crash course. Actually, call it the anti–crash course because it may help you avoid more than a few relationship collisions.

THE QUICK COURSE IN COMMITMENT

Two commitment problems are responsible for much of the energy drain in relationships. The first commitment problem is that one or both partners have not made a full commitment to the relationship itself. We refer to this problem as "having one foot out the back door." The typical pattern is that one partner is more deeply committed to the relationship than the other. When conflict arises, the deeply committed partner tries harder to solve the problem and the less committed one withdraws into less participation. If this pattern continues, the partner who tries harder ends up occupying the role of Martyr; the less committed partner becomes the Bad Boy or Bad Girl.

The second commitment problem is more pervasive. In fact,

almost everybody suffers from it. The problem: All of us have *unconscious* commitments that interfere with our conscious commitments to the relationship. In the early stage of a relationship—when romance reigns and the blood runs hot— these unconscious commitments can often stay hidden from view. As the relationship moves forward, though, the old unconscious commitments work their way to the surface to sabotage our conscious intentions. Understand how this works and you save yourself a great deal of pain and suffering. For example, we worked with a couple not long ago whose marriage had foundered after two years. Because we were familiar with the power of unconscious commitments, we were able to help them see why they were in trouble and what they needed to do to fix it.

EVEN THOUGH Paul said he was committed to his marriage, he had a stronger unconscious commitment to getting his parents' approval. His parents had never liked his choice of mates (and he ultimately realized they probably wouldn't have approved of any mate he chose). His hidden desire to please his parents kept him at arm's distance from the full embrace of his wife. This insight led to a meeting with the couple and his parents, during which a great many long-unsaid feelings were spoken. He finally declared his full commitment to Janet. He also told his parents that while he deeply loved them and wanted to please them, his marriage was more important to him than their approval. Following this emotionally charged conversation there was a palpable change in everyone in the room, like a massive sigh of relief.

Benign aftershocks reverberated through both families over the next few weeks. Much to his surprise, Paul found that his worst fear did not come true. He had been afraid his parents would withdraw, sulk, and fester with their wounded feelings. The exact opposite happened. They brought a fruit basket to Paul and Janet's house a few days after the therapy session. They told Janet that they'd been so afraid of letting go of their only son that they had never given her a chance.

Such rapid outcomes are possible only when people are courageous enough to face their unconscious commitments directly. Had Paul resisted and denied his unconscious commitment to getting his parents' approval at the expense of his marriage, the process of healing would have slowed to a crawl.

How the Process Works

The process we have developed for working through commitment problems allows their resolution to occur in a friendly and timely way. The entire process rests on an unusual principle: Relationship breakdowns are good things because they bring to light issues that need to be looked at squarely. Although a relationship breakdown is almost always caused by a hidden commitment problem, the breakdown itself is the perfect opportunity to learn how commitment really works. If the couple is courageous enough to take advantage of the opportunity, the breakdown can serve as a springboard to a new level of intimacy in the relationship.

THE WRONG KIND
OF COMMITMENT

One commitment mistake accounts for the majority of relationship pain.

In short, people commit to the wrong thing. Usually with the best of intentions, they make commitments they cannot possibly fulfill. Specifically, they commit to *outcomes*, which are beyond their control. Instead, they need to commit to *processes*, which are always within their control. Two thousand years ago Epictetus wrote a little book called *The Art of Living*, which is considered the first self-help book ever written. His opening line conveys that the secret of happiness is realizing that some things can be controlled and some cannot. Nowhere is this truth more apparent than in close relationships.

To use a familiar example, a traditional wedding vow asks us to make a commitment to "love, honor, and obey" the other person "until death do us part." This is a classic example of an outcome commitment that is doomed to failure from the start. The reason: None of us has any control over whether we will wake up loving and honoring another person tomorrow morning. Feelings by their very nature are beyond our control. What's within our control is the *process* of how we deal with our feelings. We can choose to ignore them or pay attention to them. We can choose to speak frankly about them or hide them behind closed lips. We can choose to relax our bodies to welcome them or tighten our muscles to pretend they aren't there. Some of these options obviously make for better relationships than others.

A second commitment mistake accounts for much relationship pain. This mistake is really a lack of understanding of a profound truth about commitment: All of us, at all times and in every way, are getting exactly what we're committed to getting. This discovery is usually troubling when we first see it. However, it can be one of the most liberating insights of your life. Many people come up to us after our seminars to tell us that this particular insight changed their lives more than any other they ever had. Some credit it with saving their lives.

As we said earlier, all of us have unconscious commitments that are hidden from our own view and surrounded by a wall of defenses. These hidden commitments sabotage our conscious commitments. Early in our own marriage we discovered that there is a quick and foolproof way to find out what we're really committed to: Look unflinchingly at the results we're producing. For example, even if we think we're committed to spending more quality time together, a quick look at how much quality time we're actually spending together will tell us whether we're genuinely committed to it. If we're not spending more quality time together, we have to admit that we're not actually committed to it.

Come into a session with us so you can see how these principles work in the heat of action. As you watch this drama unfold, you may think that it is moving far more quickly and easily than work with troubled relationships often does. To present a clear example of the principles, we chose a transcript in which the work does indeed proceed relatively smoothly.

As any experienced therapist knows, however, the snap-finger magic of rapid change is largely in the domain of late-night infomercials, not in the real world of normal office practice. That said, there are ways to speed up the process of change through a deep understanding of commitment. In the following example, watch closely for those moments in which we directly ask for commitments of one sort or another. Based on our experience, we believe these moments to be crucial to increasing the velocity at which couples make changes. (About

10 years ago we shifted our practice from the one-session-per-week model to what we call an intensive model. We work with people in the form of one-day or two-day intensives, during which we spend all day with the couple or individual. We've found that the intensive format allows us to accomplish in one or two days what used to take us many months.)

MARIA AND ED came to work with us for two days. Their main complaints with each other surfaced within the first few minutes, and they had a familiar ring to them. From Ed's perspective, the problem was very simple: Maria was stingy with sex. From Maria's perspective the problem didn't have anything to do with sex; the problem was emotional distance. Ed rolled his eyes—they'd been there before.

"When we were first married we made love every day," he said. "Now I'm lucky if it's every other week. That doesn't work for me."

Maria didn't sympathize at all with Ed's sexual frustration.

"I need more emotional connection with you if I'm going to get turned on. You can't go around emotionally detached all day Saturday, and then suddenly get physical with me at bedtime. When we were first together you seemed interested in me as a person, not just a body."

In helping them get out of this familiar rut, our first task is to find out if they are both committed to solving the problem. Although they've come a long way and paid a considerable fee, we need to hear a clear "yes" before we can get anything meaningful done. People come to couples counseling for many reasons other than to make discoveries about themselves that will open the flow of more love. Some have hidden agendas. They've come not to solve a problem but to prove that the marriage is really hopelessly dead. Others come trying to get us to take sides. Our way of flushing out those hidden agendas is to ask them blunt questions. Our first blunt question helps us find out if they are genuinely committed to solving the problem.

"ARE YOU WILLING to do whatever it takes to resolve these issues so you can feel more love flowing between you?"

They stared and blinked.

Ed finally broke the silence: "We're here, aren't we?" he said, a trace of irritation in his voice.

"We hear your irritation," we said, "but please note that you didn't say yes or no."

"I don't get it," he said.

Ed's an estate agent, so we used a property-selling metaphor. "Let's say you ask a couple if they want to buy the house you just showed them. They say, 'We're here, aren't we?' Would you consider that the same commitment as a 'yes' or a signature?"

He got the point. Maria's a sharp cookie—she got the point right away. Still, she couldn't resist tossing a barb in Ed's direction.

"That's the Ed I call Mr. Smart-Ass."

Noting the clenching of his jaw, we invited them to take a few deep breaths, and then we asked them our original question again.

"Are you willing to do whatever it takes to resolve these issues so you can feel more love flowing between you?"

This time they both said yes. That's all we need. It doesn't matter if they have a dozen murky agendas—practically everybody does. It doesn't matter if they have a ton of resistance. All that matters is that they go on record with a clear "yes." Making a clear commitment to do everything possible to solve the problem gives everyone a firm place to stand.

Our second blunt question: "Would you like to resolve the problem quickly or slowly?"

They quickly said, "Quickly."

Our third, and final, blunt question: "From past experience, we've found that there's one quick way to solve problems like this. It's very powerful. May we coach you with our most powerful concepts and techniques?"

Again they said, "Yes."

Now we had three commitments from them—they wanted to resolve the problem, they wanted to resolve it quickly, and they wanted us to use everything in our tool kit.

There was a perceptible change in the energy in the room. Although we were talking about heavy issues, the energy was lighter, more charged. Clear commitment has that effect—it charges the atmosphere with a kind of benign electricity.

"All right then," we said. "Let's get to work."

We asked them to face each other, with about three feet of distance between them. We asked them to make the briefest possible statement about the problem and to direct the statement to each other, not to us.

"I'm not getting enough sex," Ed said.

"I'm not getting enough emotional connection with you," Maria said.

"Okay," we said, "now we're going to use our most powerful technique to help you solve this problem. Still want us to do that?"

They answered, "Yes."

We said, "The best way to find out what you're really committed to is to observe the actual results you're producing. For example, if an alcoholic says he's committed to being sober, the best way to find out if he's really committed to it is to find out if he's had a drink recently. If he said he was committed to being sober but you found out he was still drinking, what would that make him?"

"A hypocrite," Maria said. Ed nodded.

"Maybe," we said, "but for sure it would make him a person who was more committed to drinking than to being sober."

They nodded.

"So, Ed," we said, "look Maria in the eye and declare your real commitment. Say, 'I'm committed to not getting enough sex.'"

"WHAT?" Ed's eyes practically bulged with disbelief.

We explained, "You're not getting enough sex, and the results always tell you what you're committed to, so tell her, 'Maria, I'm committed to not getting enough sex.'"

He whipped his head from side to side. "No, no, no. You don't get what I'm telling you. I'm committed to having plenty of sex. How could I be committed to not getting enough sex?"

We said, "That's a good question. Let's come back to that later. In the meantime, notice that you're avoiding doing what we've invited you to do."

"What's that?" he asked, his Mr. Smart-Ass persona back in charge.

"We invited you to look Maria in the eyes and say, 'Maria, I'm committed to not having enough sex.'"

"Even if I don't believe it?" he asked.

We nodded. "Just say it. Accent the word 'not.'"

"Maria, I'm committed to not having enough sex."

Although his face still looked puzzled and doubtful, we noted that his breathing shifted, becoming deeper and easier.

"Maria, look Ed in the eye and say, 'Ed, I'm committed to not having an emotional connection with you anymore.'"

It was clear that enlightenment had already dawned on Maria.

She nodded as she said, "Ed, I'm committed to not having an emotional connection with you anymore."

"Why?" he asked plaintively. Suddenly there was a younger tone in his voice, a kind of innocence he'd been covering over with hostility.

We said, "Let's wonder about that together. Ed, where would you have gotten the idea that you were supposed to live in a marriage where you didn't make love as often as you wanted? And Maria, where would you have gotten the idea that you were supposed to be emotionally distanced from your husband?"

Maria had already figured it out; Ed was shaking his head in puzzlement. We gave him a prompt. "Does that remind you of any relationships you saw around you growing up? Were there any people you saw frequently who complained about sexual frustration?"

He barked a sharp, bitter laugh.

"My parents fought about that constantly. I probably heard my old man bitch about his crappy sex life about five hundred times a year."

Maria chimed in with a similar observation. "My father and my brothers are all so cool and distant. Good providers, but like there's nobody home inside."

"So," we reflected back, "you learned by osmosis that marriage is supposed to be full of sexual frustration and emotional distance."

"Looks like it, doesn't it?" Ed said.

"Want to make a commitment to changing that?" we asked.

They said, "Yes."

Maria jumped in. "I make a commitment to having a lot of emotional connection in our relationship."

"Whoa," we said. "Slow down a little."

We told them that it's important to make commitments to things they have absolute control over. Nobody can control, predict, or manage their amount of emotional connection. We do, however, have control over whether we open our mouths and speak about an emotion, or whether we listen generously to our partners when they are speaking about feelings. Every one of us is in control of whether we reach over and touch our mate lovingly on the shoulder.

To bring this point to life, we invited Ed to speak a simple sentence to Maria about something he's scared or angry or hurt about.

He searched . . . and searched . . . and searched for about 30 seconds. Finally he said, "When you won't make love to me, I feel rejected."

Maria didn't respond. We invited him to communicate from a deeper place inside. "Point to where you feel rejected," we said.

He pointed to his chest.

"That's where most people feel sadness," we said. "Does that feel like an accurate description of what you're feeling?"

He nodded.

"Tell her," we suggested.

"I feel sad when you don't want to have sex with me."

"But you always get angry," Maria said.

"A lot of men do that," we said. "Men are often not very skilled at talking about tender feelings like that, so they often hide them under anger. But they can learn."

"Ed, tell her again, and this time, Maria, just listen and resonate with what he's saying."

"I feel sad when you don't want to have sex with me."

She nodded and breathed easier. Her eyes moistened slightly.

"It looks like you feel sad, too," we said.

"Yeah, that's the Ed I've been missing."

Ed and Maria made this initial shift fairly quickly. Not everyone does, of course, and even an easy first breakthrough doesn't guarantee that the second or third will be easy. In fact, subsequent work with Ed and Maria had more than a few one-step-forward-two-steps-back incidents.

On many occasions we've seen it take several hours of focused work before people softened their resistance and took responsibility for the negative results they were creating. On one memorable occasion, a deeply entrenched couple held onto their steadfast zeal to blame the other until well into the second day of the two-day intensive session. In the bigger picture, about three out of every five couples we work with experience a substantial enhancement of their relationship, with the other two muddling along slowly or dropping out entirely. Remember, too, that the couples we work with often come a long way and make a substantial monetary investment in the process. Earlier in our work, when we were using these same principles in a one-session-per-week format, we found that the velocity of change was considerably slower.

THE LARGER ISSUES

Unsettling philosophical questions are raised by the example of Ed and Maria and the techniques we employ. These questions go to the heart of how intentionality works and what drives us as human beings.

For example: Does this mean that, due to past conditioning, all of us have powerful unconscious commitments that require our partners to become the very things we complain about most bitterly? Based on our experience with thousands of couples, we can answer with a resounding "Yes." Based on dozens of experiences in nearly three decades of our own marriage, we can answer with an even more resounding "Yes."

Here's another example of how this works.

A FEW YEARS AGO we saw a couple for only an hour, but due to the

power of their commitment they were able to turn their relationship com-
pletely around in that hour. When they walked in the door they looked
like a cartoon version of a mismatched couple. He was shy and intro-
verted, an engineer who worked in the research lab of a computer firm.
She was his total opposite, an outgoing sales manager.

Their complaints about each other were true to type. According to
him, she was too loud and flirtatious at social events. According to her, he
was about as charming as "a potted plant."

We used exactly the same approach we employed in our work with
Maria and Ed. We coached him to say to her, "I'm committed to com-
plaining about your outgoing nature." She said, "I'm committed to
finding fault with your quietness." Next, we used a slightly different ques-
tion than the one we employed with Maria and Ed, but it was based on
the same principle: We all get what we're committed to getting.

The question, which we first addressed to him: "Given your pro-
gramming, why would it be inevitable that you would choose a woman
who's so outgoing?" It took him about two seconds to get the insight: "So
I could learn how to develop that side of me." He let out a big breath of
relief when he said it.

We addressed the question to her. "Given your early programming,
why would it be inevitable that you'd draw a quiet guy into your life, and
then complain about his quietness?" She told us that her parents had
played out the same dynamic throughout her childhood. "Believe it or
not," she said, "my dad's an electrical engineer, too."

"So, what is the inspired reason you chose a guy like Dave?"

"So I could cultivate my quiet, meditative side."

They nailed it. Each of us has certain learning needs that
propel us into our relationships and influence the kind of mate
we choose. Then most of us promptly forget that we've chosen

our mates for a reason. Instead of embracing them as a learning ally, we shoulder them as a burdensome improvement project. When they resist our self-improvement scheme for them (and they almost always do), we grow resentful. We also fail to get the advantage of meeting the learning need that caused us to pull that particular mate into our life in the first place.

THE DIFFERENCE BETWEEN PHILOSOPHY AND REALITY

We should make it very clear that our experience with unconscious intentions is based on helping real couples work out real problems. It's not based on a philosophical principle or some theory we're trying to concoct. Based on our clinical experience, we believe that all of us enter our intimate relationships with unconscious intentions, and those hidden intentions eventually override the conscious and noble intentions with which we began the relationship.

Does this mean that human beings are responsible for creating all the bad things that happen to them?

Our answer is a resounding "No."

Can human beings *claim* responsibility for bad things that happen to them and learn a lot about themselves by doing so?

Yes—we've seen hundreds of such examples change hundreds of lives for the better. We'll show you what we mean in chapter 4.

Now, refer to the Action Plan for the practical application of the commitment material from this chapter.

If you're experiencing commitment

issues that require emergency

assistance,

turn to page 203, and then

turn to page 234.

Your Action Plan

Your Commitment

"I commit to learning from all my interactions and from the results of my actions."

Say this to yourself to make sure you're in agreement with it inside. Say it to your partner, and listen to him or her say it to you. If your partner isn't an active player in the process of transforming the relationship, you can simply work with the material yourself until she or he gets on board.

Your Ongoing Practice

When you aren't feeling good inside, or when something is not going well in the relationship, claim that you're committed to the very thing that is not going well. For example, if you and your partner fight a lot, you're committed to fighting. If people leave you, you're committed to being abandoned. What doesn't work is to pretend this isn't happening or to pretend you didn't mean what you said or did. That move makes people crazy. The power move locates you at the root of the problem so you can actually free the energy you've been recycling in your unconscious commitment.

Acknowledge and name the unconscious commitment. Say it out loud several times until you can breathe freely while stating this unconscious commitment. "Hmmm, I must be committed to feeling this way." "Hmmm, I must be committed to things going this way."

In the second part of radical commitment you shape a new conscious commitment based on what you really want. Once you've freed up your attachment to things not going well, you can create a new commitment that can guide your life in a chosen direction. Then you can steer your course by recommitting to this new path when you drift. Make your commitment active by starting the sentence, "I commit . . . "

Here are some examples:

Unconscious commitment: I'm committed to being criticized.
New conscious commitment: I commit to generating curiosity when I receive feedback.

Unconscious commitment: I'm committed to not being listened to.
New conscious commitment: I commit to speaking in a way that generates interest.

Unconscious commitment: I'm committed to conflict.
New conscious commitment: I commit to fully appreciating myself and my partner.

Your Ten-Second Technique

When you feel off-track in yourself or your relationship, take a deep breath and acknowledge, "This is what I'm committed to right now." Then stretch and breathe while literally changing your direction. Move your body in a new direction while saying to yourself, "I commit to going in a new, positive direction."

CHAPTER 3

The Second Secret

A New Way of Being with Emotions

ONE moment of emotional transparency can work miracles in a relationship. We know that beyond a shadow of a doubt. Not only have we witnessed hundreds of such miracles in our practice, we're direct beneficiaries in our own marriage. We probably wouldn't be married today, and we're sure we wouldn't be writing this book, if it weren't for a moment of emotional transparency early in our relationship. We were heading along a path to disaster when a simple miracle occurred that put us on the right track again. More than twenty years later we continue to reap the rewards of this special moment.

GAY: One of my most troublesome unconscious patterns was my habit of finding fault and criticizing the woman I was with. My Critic had been a factor in the eventual dissolution of three major relationships and many minor ones. Although I wanted desperately not to have it mess up my growing relationship with Kathlyn, I couldn't seem to stop the habit. By the time I would become aware of a critical comment, the words were already out of my mouth. One of John F. Kennedy's friends once asked him why he continued to engage in flagrant sexual infidelities at the possible expense of getting caught, losing his reputation, and even risking his health. JFK replied, "I can't help it." That's how I felt about my critical comments.

KATHLYN: Being on the receiving end of Gay's criticism was painful, but I couldn't find any way to make it stop, either. He's brilliant and articulate with words, so that when he would criticize me I would usually feel that I actually was at fault. My father is exactly the same way, and I'm convinced I was originally drawn to Gay partly because I needed to work out this issue of being around critical men.

GAY: One Friday evening Katie was late coming home. She'd told me she was coming home around 7:30, and when she walked in the door at 8:15 I didn't even pause to say "hello" before I started in on her. The fact that she was carrying two grocery bags didn't even make an impression on me, so intent was I on criticizing her for being late. However, something magical happened that evening that changed our lives permanently.

THE EMOTIONAL UNDERPINNINGS
OF A PATTERN

Before we tell you about the magic moment, take a minute to understand why patterns like chronic criticism persist. Usually, there is some hidden emotion under the pattern that keeps it in place, even if the person consciously wants to change the pattern. When the concealed feeling comes to light, the pattern loses its underpinnings and is much easier to change. Emotional awareness and transparency provide the drop of solvent that unglues long-stuck patterns.

GAY: I got about three sentences into my criticism of Katie for being late. Suddenly I became aware of a sensation in my body . . . . a sensation I realized was always in the background when the urge came over me to criticize someone. I paused in midcriticism and tuned in to what I was feeling. It was a queasy-butterfly sensation in my belly. It was fear.

Up until that moment of new emotional awareness, I always felt I was justifiably angry when I criticized someone. The problem was simple and obvious: They had done something wrong and I was therefore mad about it. They needed to hear what they'd done wrong so they wouldn't do it again. My view of everything changed in that moment, however, when I felt the fear in my belly. I suddenly realized that my pattern of criticism was not driven by anger at all. I was scared.

I blurted this out to Katie, and she put down the grocery bags to come and put her arm around me. I tuned in more deeply to the queasy-butterfly sensation. I was scared, but what was I scared about? The answer came quickly, with a flood of awareness and memories. I was afraid of losing her. I was afraid of being abandoned, left behind.

I spoke all this to Katie, and a puzzled look came over her face. She said she didn't have any intention of going away or leaving me behind.

"I know," I said. "This doesn't have anything to do with you."

I'll never forget the look of relief that washed over her face as she realized that all my criticisms had nothing to do with her.

We sat down on the spot and talked for over an hour about our respective roles in the pattern. We saw clearly how my urge to criticize her interlocked perfectly with her lifelong feeling that she had done something wrong.

By the end of that hour I knew myself better than I ever had. It was a very practical kind of self-knowledge because it stopped my pattern of criticizing in its tracks. I realized that the pattern was rooted in a fear of being abandoned, based on some real experiences that befell me in my first year of life. I was afraid of being left, so when a woman got close to me I'd start criticizing her so she wouldn't get any closer. If I let anybody get really close to me, it would hurt much worse when she eventually left me.

KATHLYN: That conversation changed my life. I realized that I'd carried around a feeling of being wrong ever since I could remember. No wonder critical men kept showing up in my life! I was a criticism-waiting-to-happen! Down underneath my need to be criticized was a feeling of fear that was very similar to what Gay described. We were both afraid of being abandoned. He expressed it through criticizing, and I expressed it through feeling wrong—I would try harder to be good and maybe they wouldn't leave me.

EMOTIONAL TRANSPARENCY

Moments of emotional transparency change lives. It's even better, though, when emotional transparency becomes a daily habit. Then, you can live on a steady diet of miracles day in and day out.

After powerful moments of emotional awareness in therapy sessions, many couples have remarked, "It's so simple!" But it's only simple when viewed from the present looking backward. We stayed in the grip of the criticism pattern for years before we broke through it. Now, of course, it seems obvious how it all worked, but viewed from within the pattern it was anything but easy.

Ten Seconds to Vitality

We have seen hundreds of examples of something we would never have believed unless we had personally witnessed it: long-dead marriages being brought to life by ten seconds of emotional transparency. When we first began working with couples we had no idea of the extent to which people will go to conceal emotions they desperately want to avoid feeling or expressing. Many people will sacrifice the relationship itself to avoid sharing an emotional intimacy that would literally take ten seconds to say.

There are three main feelings that cause most of the trouble in long-term relationships; anger, grief, and fear. It's never the feelings themselves that are the problem—it's our unwillingness to confront them in ourselves and talk about them to others. To make it easier, we have developed a simple but comprehensive road map that can be taught to any couple in less than an hour.

Here is an example of that road map at work.

A WELL-KNOWN COUPLE visited our office to give their marriage one last chance. Their twenty-five-year union now felt like a "prison of lead" to them. His complaint was that she had changed from the woman he had originally married. Where had the "sweet, cooperative" woman gone? Where had she turned into a "raging critaholic"? She complained that he was uncommunicative, boring, and materialistic. "When I met him he didn't even watch TV. Now all he can think about is getting a bigger one."

A few seconds of emotional transparency, however, sent a bolt of vitality through them that they hadn't felt in years. They resisted mightily for an hour or so, using a defensive barrage of interrupting each other, contemptuous sneers, and long-winded justifications. Finally, though, their defenses melted when one of them had the courage to reveal a truth that had gone unspoken for too long. The magic sentence was simple: "I don't think I love you anymore. I've been haunted by that feeling for years but I couldn't quite get it out of my mouth."

Although this admission sounds like a terrible thing to say or to hear, the act of revealing it liberated the speaker to feel an upsurge of love. In fact, within seconds of saying it, he suddenly realized he loved his wife deeply. He also realized that the real issue had nothing to do with her.

His courageous revelation opened the door to a wellspring of hidden feelings, desires, and aspirations for both of them. At the end of it, though, it was all about creativity. She felt squelched under a load of domestic responsibilities at home while also feeling overworked in her career. She would leave the office exhausted only to arrive home knowing that she couldn't meet the unnamed expectations of her husband and his parents (who lived next door).

He had his own version of the same issues. He felt that he had sacrificed every ounce of his own creative energy in order to fulfill his family responsibilities. To their great credit, this couple shed the burden of this excess baggage to make a mutual commitment to their individual creativity and to learn a new language of authentic feeling.

WORKING WONDERS
FOR YOURSELF

Now, let's find out how you can create these kinds of miracles for yourself. First, we'll explore exactly what it means to be emotionally transparent and why it produces such miraculous results in close relationships.

What Emotional Transparency Means

Emotional transparency is the ability to know your own feelings and to talk about them so that others clearly understand them. At the other end of the continuum is emotional opaqueness—you do not know how you feel and cannot talk about your feelings so that people understand them.

In close relationships, much damage is done by emotional opaqueness, the inability or unwillingness to discuss feelings openly. Sometimes the damage is done willfully: Some people refuse to look into their feelings or talk about them clearly so that they can punish others. They use their hidden emotions as a weapon. Much of the time, though, people are unable to discuss their feelings because of a lack of information and a lack of practice. After all, compared to the amount of time we spend in school on math or science, how much training did any of us get in the art of emotional communication?

Suppose you ask your mate, "What are you feeling right now?" Emotional transparency is the ability to check inside, then say, "I'm afraid" or "I'm angry" or "I'm feeling very close to you right now." Emotional opaqueness is when your mate won't look inside or doesn't know how. Emotional opaqueness is, "I don't know" or "I'm not feeling anything."

Why Emotional Transparency Works Wonders

When human beings are breathing, they are also feeling. When human beings are eating, they are also feeling. Awake or asleep, at work or at play, we are all feeling, all the time. In the background of all human experience is the rich play of emotion and sensation.

If you were to compare the logical, thinking part of the brain to the emotional, feeling part, you would see a huge difference. The feeling part is the size of the juicy part of a grapefruit—the thinking part is the size of the rind. Early in our lives, we use the "rind" of reason to keep our feelings from seeping out in ways that get us in trouble. Later, however, the very rind that protected us becomes a barrier that keeps our emotions sealed within. In order to experience genuine intimacy, we absolutely must reveal our emotions to those we care about.

Like a picture window, the window to our emotions needs to be polished daily. This daily window cleaning is one of the major disciplines of intimacy. If we can see clearly into our own emotions, we reveal ourselves to ourselves. When we can speak about our emotions clearly to people we care about, we reveal ourselves to them. Herein lies the power of emotional transparency: *The act of revealing our feelings to ourselves and to others frees the energy that previously was bound up in the effort to keep those feelings hidden.*

It requires energy—literal physical energy—to hide our emotions from ourselves. It requires even more energy to conceal them from others. And the truth is, nobody ever hides anything. People who think they're hiding their anger reveal it through chronic headaches. People who think they're hiding their fear reveal it through stomach trouble. The mind can lie, but the aching head and the upset stomach speak the truth.

Emotional transparency is simple but it's hardly ever easy. To know how we feel is to know what's real, and it is often much more seductive to live in illusion rather than face the simple reality of our feelings.

In our work we've had the experience of helping many people learn to talk openly about their feelings to people they care about. We've often marveled at the lengths to which people will go to hide their true feelings.

Why is this? What's so hard about saying simple things like, "I felt hurt when you said that" or "I'm afraid you'll leave me and I'll be all alone"? The answer is that most of us, as we grow up, attach ourselves to a particular image of ourselves, and this image becomes more important to us than reality.

GAY: As a little boy growing up in the John Wayne era of the fifties, I learned a lot of macho attitudes like, "Big boys don't cry" and "No pain, no gain." In my neighborhood these attitudes worked pretty well. Acting tough, like nothing bothered you, was the accepted way to be in that part of the world. Along with this studied nonchalance went an attitude of "I can handle everything myself." When I was upset about something, I hid it carefully inside. The last thing I would do was tell somebody else how I was feeling. Later on, though, in the real world of close relationships, those attitudes cost me more than I could ever have imagined. In close relationships, I found I needed to let down my defenses and admit the reality of my feelings. It took me years to learn how to drop my defensiveness long enough to admit that I was hurt or that something bothered me.

HOW TO MAKE IT EASIER

Although it's not easy to let people see how we feel, there are ways to make it easier. Ideally we would all be taught useful skills like emotional awareness in elementary school, right alongside long division, reading, and the state capitals. Most of us weren't fortunate enough to go to that kind of elementary school, though, so we have to play catch-up as adults. We have to start exactly where we are, wherever we are.

Begin with Commitment

The best starting place we've found is with a commitment to emotional transparency. A commitment won't guarantee that you will always be emotionally transparent with each other, but it will give you a firm place to stand in your quest for lasting love.

Try on the following commitment:

I commit to knowing all my feelings and speaking truthfully about them to people I care about.

If you were meeting with us in our office, we would ask you to face your partner and to speak this commitment sincerely to each other. We would ask you to say it several times until you felt the sincerity of your commitment in your body and mind.

It's natural to feel various types of resistance come up in yourself when you make this commitment. The most common type of resistance is confusion and ignorance. People say, "I'd like to commit to that but I don't have the slightest idea how I'd make good on it." Don't let the lack of know-how stop you from making the commitment, though, because a sincere commitment will actually begin to draw to you the tools and skills you need. Without the commitment, you won't turn on the mechanisms that start the flow of awareness within you.

It's also natural and normal for one partner to be more committed to emotional transparency than the other. Many people would argue that it's a man/woman thing: Men are more resistant to emotional transparency than women. We've worked with several hundred same-sex couples, however, and there's usually one partner who's more committed than the other to emotional transparency.

THE ESSENTIAL SKILLS

Once you're committed to emotional transparency, what do you need to know to make good on your commitment?

There are only two skills, both incredibly simple, that will help you become more committed to emotional transparency. Due largely to societal programming, however, both are incredibly challenging to master.

The first skill: Know what you're feeling.

The second skill: Speak the simple truth about it.

The First Skill

From our practical experience, we can tell you that the first skill of emotional transparency involves four things:

* Knowing when you're scared

* Knowing when you're angry

* Knowing when you're sad

* Knowing when you have sexual desires

Those aren't the only four feelings, of course, but they are the four feelings that cause the most trouble when we hide them from ourselves or from people we care about. Learn to recognize your inner signals of fear, anger, sadness, and sexual desire, and you give yourself an emotional vocabulary that will help you resolve relationship conflict much more quickly.

The Second Skill

The second skill of emotional transparency is speaking simply about those four feelings to people you care about. It's learning to say simple truths like "I'm scared" and "I'm angry" to people you want to be close to. It's learning to speak the emotional truths of your life in such a way that the people you care for don't have to wonder what you're actually feeling.

Focus on talking about your feelings to people you care about. If you don't care much about a particular person, you can still speak truthfully about your feelings, but it's not essential. With people you care about, though, it's absolutely essential that you know your feelings and speak truthfully about them. Emotional honesty brings people closer together.

We make a point of saying that these two skills are based on our practical experience. In other words, we're not laying out a theory of emotional transparency here. We're highlighting the two skills that real couples have found essential in getting unstuck from vitality-sapping patterns. These are the two skills that bring back passion and creativity to long-term relationships.

BARRIERS
TO EMOTIONAL DISCOVERY

The moment you commit to being aware of your feelings and speaking truthfully about them, you come up against powerful societal forces opposed to your commitment. The entire advertising industry is one of the major barriers you face. Manufacturers of many products have a big interest in keeping us in the dark about our emotions. This allows them to play on our emotions to sell us things.

Watch a few hours of television and you'll see what we mean. You'll see good buddies enjoying warm camaraderie . . . made possible by cold beer. You'll see nerdy guys with beautiful women . . . in the nerdy guy's hot new car. Open a magazine in which perfume or aftershave is advertised and look at the images used to sell them. The images often say, "Wear this and you'll fit in with the cool people—you won't be a loser anymore!" Watch how cigarettes are marketed in movies. The actors light up at moments of peak emotional intensity. The message is clear to young moviegoers everywhere: This is the way cool people deal with their emotions.

The powerfully persuasive (and powerfully expensive) messages of advertising are aimed directly at our emotions: Buy our products to feel happy and safe. Buy our products to avoid feeling fear, loneliness, and the pain of loss. Buy our products to be part of the in-crowd. These images and messages have a powerful negative effect on our ability to develop emotional transparency. For example, part of emotional transparency is the ability to resolve our feelings with our own natural resources: to soothe our fears with a few deep breaths, to let ourselves cry in response to grief, to understand what's eating away at us (rather than eating it away).

Religious programming can also be a barrier to emotional awareness. As we write this book, for example, the Roman Catholic Church is in the midst of a huge and costly scandal, which on one level is about the sexual abuse of children by priests. On a more fundamental level, however, it's really about lying. It's about whether people in positions of power lie to protect the interests of the bureaucracy or speak the truth to protect the interests of children. We don't know yet whether children will continue to be sacrificed for the bureaucracy's sake or whether the bureaucracy can become flexible enough to accommodate the truth. Religious concepts erect mental barriers against the development of emotional transparency. Part of emotional intelligence involves the ability to acknowledge and embrace deep feelings. When mental concepts are instilled at an early age, it prevents the natural inquiry into those deeper emotions.

Advertising and religion are but two of the powerful forces you face when you make a commitment to emotional awareness and transparency. There are others. For example, you may find people in your immediate and extended family who do not want you to feel what you feel and speak the truth about it. We once facilitated a family-therapy session in which the "problem child," the middle of seven children, said she had often felt unloved and unaccepted by the others. The eldest angrily snapped, "You couldn't possibly have felt that!" There was a long silence during which everyone in the room realized that we had just heard a living example of what the middle daughter had spoken of.

Regardless of the barrier, though, your commitment to knowing and speaking the truth about your feelings eventually has to become bigger than the societal forces against it. We all need to become aware of our feelings so that they can work for us rather than be used against us by the forces of society, such as advertising, or the repressive intentions of people around us. Nowhere is this more true than in close relationships.

BARRIERS TO TRUTH-TELLING

We've focused on the barriers to knowing our emotions, but when we commit to speaking truthfully about them we encounter obstacles that are perhaps even tougher to surmount. After all, how many hours of your schooling were devoted to showing you how to speak articulately about your feelings? Unless you're lucky to have gone to an uncommonly progressive school, the answer is zero. Personally speaking, we went all the way to university before the subject was introduced.

In addition to sheer ignorance, there are stiff prohibitions against speaking the truth about important matters. You've probably heard proverbs such as, "The truth hurts" and "Some things are better left unsaid." Almost everyone has heard those, but how many of us have heard, "Truth heals" or "Don't ever leave anything important unsaid"?

Getting hit on the head with a mallet probably hurts more if you resist it, but it still hurts if you accept it calmly. Truth is different because it's made up only of puffs of air. The truth only hurts when we resist it. We've been in many rooms when difficult truths have been spoken, even truths like, "You have terminal cancer" and "I've been having an affair with your best friend." Whether truth hurts depends entirely on how much resistance we mount against seeing and hearing the reality of it. We've seen people accept a terminal diagnosis with a sigh of relief. We've also seen people greet an "I'm having an affair . . . " truth with the same kind of relief, as in, "Now everything I've been feeling makes sense."

Naturally, we've seen the opposite, too. We've been with people as they exploded in anger or stormed out of the room when truths have been revealed. It all has to do with how much resistance we've built up to seeing things exactly as they are.

Does It Matter How Truth Is Delivered?

On the surface you might think that whether "truth hurts" depends on how it's delivered. In actual fact, though, it never does. What matters is whether what's being delivered is actually the truth. If we say to you, "You're an idiot," you could rightfully argue that we've delivered a truth in a hurtful way. In fact, though, we haven't delivered the truth at all. "You're an idiot" is an opinion or an interpretation—it's a long way from the truth. The truth can never be argued about. The truth beneath "You're an idiot" may be something like, "I felt hurt when you started dating my ex-spouse." Whatever it is, it's always something unarguable. Nothing else counts as truth, and no other kind of truth heals.

The Big Payoff

You become a hero in your own life the moment you commit to knowing your feelings and speaking about them honestly. In your relationships you become the trailblazer rather than the trailer. You become the place where truth is born, not the place where it goes to die. There is an intrinsic satisfaction to taking a stand for truth in a world where it's in such short supply. The rewards don't stop there, though.

Becoming the source of truth is a reward you can feel and enjoy immediately in your own body. You get an instant surge of vitality each time you acknowledge the truth and speak about it simply. If it's a truth you've been carrying for a while, the feeling of releasing it is like suddenly shedding a heavy load you've been carrying on your shoulders. You feel a joyful relief, and you also become aware of the burden you've been carrying. The next time you get the urge to withhold a significant truth, you think twice because you remember the heaviness of it.

CONSCIOUS LISTENING

How you listen shapes how people talk to you. In the early days of our relationship, before we'd learned the importance of conscious listening, we often had interchanges like this one:

KATHLYN: I'm feeling kind of tired and stressed out today.

GAY: Why don't you take some time tomorrow and go out into the mountains?

KATHLYN: Umm . . . thanks. I'll think about it.

What's wrong with this interchange? On the surface it sounds like Gay made a positive, helpful suggestion. It's a classic example, however, of what we call a listening filter. At a more extreme level we call them listening shields.

A listening filter hears what's said through the filter of the listener's preferences and prejudices. It doesn't attempt to get inside the speaker's experience.

Let's go through the interchange again, in slow motion. First, Kathlyn says she's tired and stressed out. Gay responds with a suggestion of how she can fix the problem. This particular filter was one of our most popular ones: listening to fix. Not only did he try to fix the problem, he applied a "fix" that comes from inside his experience.

GAY: When I'm tired and stressed out, I like to take some alone time to recharge my batteries. I like spending some time communing with nature, taking a walk in solitude or sometimes simply sitting on a rock by a stream for an hour or two.

KATHLYN: I like to recharge by being around people more than Gay does. For me, having a cup of tea with a friend is incredibly nurturing.

There are other listening filters that we found ourselves using out of habit:

- Listening to find fault: "How could you be tired and stressed out? You really haven't done all that much this week."

- Listening to rebut: "I don't think you're really tired and stressed out—you're just upset you couldn't go skiing last weekend."

- Listening to minimize: "You don't look that tired to me."

- Listening to compare: "*You're* tired and stressed out! What about me?"

On the surface it might sound simple to avoid using your listening filters. We found it devilishly hard, though . . . a skill that required much practice. Since those early days we've taught the skills to thousands of people, and they haven't found them easy to learn, either. It's well worth the investment because it's the only way to get to know another person at deeper levels.

What Does Conscious Listening Sound Like?

Let's run the original interchange again, removing the listening filters and using the skills of conscious listening.

KATHLYN: I'm feeling kind of tired and stressed out.

GAY: Mmm, I can hear that in your voice. What are you experiencing?

KATHLYN: My shoulders are achy and I'm running a lot of worry-thoughts through my mind.

GAY: Have you noticed if it's about something specific, or is it more of a general kind of thing?

KATHLYN: One thing that keeps running through my mind is how we're going to pay for Chris's orthodontics and have anything left over for Christmas.

GAY: Want to talk about that for a while?

KATHLYN: Yes, let's do some brainstorming . . . but I think I'm going to take a hot bath first.

Conscious listening comes from an intention to tune in to the speaker's experience and draw out from him or her as much as he or she would like to share. Conscious listening avoids imposing the listener's experience on the speaker unless it's asked for. Herein lies the reason it's so hard to do. In the heat of conflict, none of us feels that our point of view is being considered. When stress levels get cranked up, most of us feel that our experience is being slighted or downright ignored. Yet, that's the very moment when a few seconds of conscious listening can make great strides toward restoring harmony.

Remember, we didn't say it was easy! Without a strong, sincere commitment, though, it's practically impossible. The starting place, then, is for both people in the relationship to make a commitment to conscious listening. You can still make progress if only one person is committed, but it makes for slower going.

THE FARTHER REACHES OF TRANSPARENCY

In our experience, absolute honesty is a powerful force for good in any close relationship. Going further, we believe that complete transparency is the best aphrodisiac ever discovered, as well as the best way to get a good night's sleep.

The big payoff for transparency is the flow of vital energy and the simultaneous feeling of harmonious ease. That's the positive side. On the flip side, dishonesty and opaqueness destroy the flow of intimacy and probably cause more impotence and orgasmic dysfunction than alcohol. If there is any significant truth you haven't communicated to your primary partner, you forfeit the right to expect a good relationship with him or her. Most people don't know this simple principle, so when things aren't going well in the relationship, they blame the other person. Inside ourselves, though, should be our first place to look: If you don't feel sexually turned on by your partner, or if you're having trouble getting a good night's sleep, you're likely to have hidden a truth that needs to be brought out into the open.

Here are the most popular examples of hidden truths:

- I've had sexual experiences I haven't told you about.

- I've spent money you don't know about.

- I've got (an illegitimate child, herpes, a secret bank account, etc.) and I haven't told you about it.

- I'm still angry about. . .

- I'm still hurt about. . .

- I'm scared about. . .

- I really want . . . and I'm afraid to tell you.

Most people tell us they haven't been honest with their partners because "my partner really doesn't want to hear the truth" or because "I don't want to hurt my partner." When they get under these superficial reasons, the reason usually turns out to be, "I haven't told the truth because I don't want to face the consequences." Under that, however, is the real reason: "I haven't told the truth because I fear living at the highest level of creativity and energy, and lying is one way I know to dampen my energy."

People tell us that they dread telling the truth because they fear the consequences. In actual fact, though, we've seen honesty produce only positive consequences in the long run. There is usually a short-term flurry or upset when a person shares a withheld truth, but the ultimate outcome is usually a more stable relationship.

THE ACID TEST

Here's the best question we've ever found to assess the health of a relationship:

"Have I discussed anything *significant* with a third party that I haven't talked directly to my partner about?" For example, have you told a friend or a therapist about an infidelity but not your partner? When we have secrets, we forfeit the right to expect genuine intimacy. Intimacy can occur only in a secret-free relationship. Plus, as every experienced relationship counselor can tell you, the more a person complains about a partner, the more secrets the complainer is likely to be harboring. When people keep secrets from their partners, they have to keep finding more and more faults about them. In the twisted thinking of the secret-keeper, the secrets are justified because of the faults and flaws of the other person.

Tips on Communicating Significant Withheld Truths

Here are some ways you can make truth-telling much more positive for all concerned:

- Don't do it while you or your partner are driving, operating kitchen equipment, or at any other time when an upset could cause physical injury.

- Don't use liquor or other drugs to loosen yourself up beforehand. This sends the wrong message to your body—that you can't be honest unless you're chemically altered. Our bodies need to know that they can be honest all the time.

- Don't think it has anything to do with the other person. If you've been thinking the other person "isn't safe" or "doesn't want to hear it," you're missing the point. It's really about you and your fear of living at your highest level of integrity and positive energy.

PREPARING TO TAKE
THESE INSIGHTS INTO REAL LIFE

The first step to making these insights real is to make a two-pronged commitment. To become emotionally transparent, we all need to make a commitment to knowing our feelings, sharing our feelings, and hearing the feelings of others. It's a commitment to seeing and saying what's real, combined with a commitment to hearing what's real in the other person's experience. Here are two commitments we ask people to make in the early stages of our work with them. These commitments open the doorway to a world of gentle but powerful changes in a relationship.

I commit to letting all my feelings be seen, heard, and appreciated.
I commit to seeing, hearing, and appreciating all the feelings of others.

You might think it odd to use verbs like "seen" and "seeing" in regard to feelings. Most people probably think of feelings as something you talk about with your mouth and hear with your ears. More than 90 percent of feelings, however, are communicated through our body language, and this visible language can be seen before any spoken version of our feelings. In order to hear what's really going on, first you have to "listen with your eyes" to *see* what's really going on. A raised eyebrow or a clenched jaw muscle speaks eloquently about your feelings, usually long before your conscious mind can organize a spoken communication about them. The trick is for both people in a relationship to learn to appreciate that eloquence and turn it into an ally.

It might also seem odd to see the word "appreciating" in the commitment. Most of us, when we're stuck, don't feel very appreciative toward our feelings or anybody else's. Here, though, we're using "appreciate" in the sense of "being sensitive and aware of . . . " A person who appreciates art has cultivated the skill of being sensitive and aware of the subtleties of art. In this spirit, we all need to become sensitive and aware of the subtleties of feeling.

Delivering the Message

One of the package delivery companies used to have a slogan that went something like, "When you absolutely, positively have to get it there on time." In all the relationship-coaching sessions we've conducted, it's been incredibly important to deliver emotional communications in ways that produce harmony rather than conflict. This experience has allowed us to develop a way of delivering emotional "packages" when you absolutely, positively have to get the message understood clearly.

In emotional communication, simple is good. The simplest, clearest way to talk about your feelings is to begin with what we call a one-breath statement. One-breath statements take only one breath to deliver. In clock time it's only a few seconds, and that's plenty long enough for most important communications. Here are a few examples:

- "I'm angry right now."

- "I still feel hurt and sad."

- "I'm scared about giving the speech this afternoon."

The second step to making these insights real is to get comfortable with delivering one-breath statements about the key feelings that come up in close relationships. Remember, the Big Three are anger, fear, and sadness or grief.

With this essential background information in mind, now let's get specific. Your Action Plan on the next page will show you exactly how to make emotional transparency a positive force in your moment-by-moment life.

Your Action Plan

Your Commitment

"I commit to speaking and listening to you in a way that celebrates essence."

Your Ongoing Practice

Get feedback from your partner at a time when you are both willing to learn. Ask each other, "When I'm operating on automatic, what is the way in which I most often listen to you?" Do your best to simply receive the answer, whether it's listening to fix, to criticize, to analyze, whatever. The following day, release that automatic way of listening by taking off those particular metaphorical earmuffs whenever your partner is speaking to you. Whenever you are listening, consciously practice appreciating what your partner is saying. That is, be sensitively aware of the unique form of this communication. Wonder about the feelings embedded in the words and the desires that may lie between the words.

Your Ten-Second Technique

Whenever you are experiencing a conflict or dis-ease with your partner, make this following move first. Notice any body sensations in your shoulders, chest area, or around your navel. Take a deep, relaxed breath and describe those sensations in a one-breath statement. Eventually you may get sensitive enough to identify the stomach sensations as fear, the shoulder tightening as anger, and the chest constriction as sadness. In the beginning, though, just report the body sensation by saying something like, "My stomach is getting tight right now." These simple statements have a powerful impact when you deliver them to your partner.

If you feel your partner is lying,

turn to page 197 to find out

how to know for sure.

If you need emergency help

telling a difficult truth,

turn to page 210.

CHAPTER 4

The Third Secret

*The No-Blame Relationship and
How to Create It*

Can you imagine a close relationship in which neither person criticizes the other? Can you picture how a marriage might operate if blame and criticism simply did not occur?

Those questions first circulated through our minds in 1981, just before we were married. As part of our premarital preparations, we sat down together for an hour or two every week for about two months prior to our wedding. During those hours we spent a lot of time imagining the kind of relationship we wanted to create. It was then that we had our first glimmers of a no-blame relationship. At the time it seemed like a distant possibility at best, an Everest hidden in the clouds. We were inspired to take the challenge, though, and we're very glad we did.

It began, as every heroic task must, with a single step: commitment. As part of our wedding vows we made a special kind of commitment to each other. We held hands and looked each other in the eyes and made a commitment to ending blame and criticism in our relationship. It took several years of intense focus to make good on our commitment, but eventually we did it. It's been many years now since either one of us has blamed the other for anything, and we haven't missed it the slightest bit.

We took up the challenge of ending blame and criticism for several reasons. Both of us were familiar with the research studies that show the destructive effects of blame and criticism in close relationships, but that's not the main reason we wanted to create a blame-free zone in our home. The main reason was much more personal: We come from two of the most critical families you'd ever be likely to meet. They're wonderful people—they just can't stop criticizing each other. We found ourselves falling into the same pattern of constant criticism in the early days of our relationship. One fine day, however, we caught ourselves in midcriticism and sat down for a talk.

That conversation changed our lives radically. We decided that enough was enough. Without question, our respective families had perfected the art of chronic blame and criticism. There were no further improvements to be made in that particular art form. So, we decided to do everything we could to end the pattern of chronic blame and criticism in our generation. If our children wanted to pick up blame and criticism again, that was their choice, *but they wouldn't learn it from us.* We decided to focus instead on mastering the art of chronic appreciation (see chapter 6).

CLAIMING RESPONSIBILITY

First, though, how do we end blame? As we said in chapter 2, we aren't responsible for creating all the bad things that happen to us. But we can claim responsibility for the bad things that happen and learn a lot about ourselves by doing so. It all depends on whether you think of responsibility as something you are or as something you do. For us, the only useful way of thinking about responsibility is as something we do. We use an operational definition of responsibility, not a theoretical one: Responsibility is an action you take, not a quality that can be assigned. A judge and jury can assign responsibility to a criminal for an act, but that criminal's life will not begin to change until he or she makes a conscious choice to *take* responsibility. If you go into a prison you will quickly find out how useless it is to assign responsibility. Few of the prisoners claim any responsibility for any of the crimes they've been convicted for.

Meaningful responsibility can never be assigned from outside. Even well-meaning, metaphysically inclined people are woefully unclear about the issue of responsibility. At lectures people frequently ask questions such as, "Are people responsible for what happens to them when they're children?" or "Do we choose our parents?" Some metaphysical systems teach that people reincarnate to learn certain lessons, and they choose those childhood experiences that facilitate what they are here to learn.

To us, that point of view seems absurd. If a drunken father comes home and beats up his eight-year-old, it's ridiculous to speculate that the eight-year-old is in some way responsible. If that same child, however, comes to therapy twenty years later, complaining of a pattern of troubled interactions with male authority figures, he or she can solve the problem more quickly by taking full responsibility for perpetuating those situations in his or her adult life. The key point is this: There is tremendous healing power in taking responsibility for something right now in the present, but no healing value in looking back to the past to blame yourself or anyone else.

Similarly, if you get a sore throat or a stomachache a couple times a year, it's probably not worthwhile for you to spend much energy wondering if those illnesses are psychosomatic. If, however, you see a pattern—perhaps the sore throat or stomachache tends to occur on mornings when a speech is to be given later that day—then it would definitely be worthwhile for you to take responsibility for creating it.

As one of our witty students has said, "All the best responsibility is taken."

Speaking from practical experience, as well as from philosophical inclination, we always advocate that each person in a given situation takes 100 percent responsibility for creating the situation. There is a possibility of meaningful resolution only when everyone does rigorous self-inquiry into how and why he or she might have created the situation. A power struggle flares up the moment one person or the other retreats even to 99 percent responsibility. If one person identifies him/herself as the victim, the other person immediately does so, too. From this perspective of victimhood, the other person always looks like the perpetrator. We've seen these "I'm-a-bigger-victim-than-you-are" power struggles go on for decades.

Let's leave victimization claims to the lawyers. As real people dealing with the real problems of everyday life, we can take a genuinely empowering new direction. We can choose to see a world of people who are seeking to take full responsibility for their lives. We can choose to operate from a place of radical responsibility: In every moment of life, we get exactly what we're committed to getting. From this place of reclaimed power, we can choose conscious new commitments that are un-fettered by the past and that make us free to act powerfully in the present.

None of us will do this perfectly. Ultimately it is the act of recommitting that has as much to do with the healing process as the original conscious commitment. For example, think back to Ed and Maria from chapter 2. They committed to speaking clearly about their emotions and listening generously to each other when they spoke.

MAKING THAT conscious commitment initiated a process of change, but it certainly didn't guarantee it. In fact, they violated this fresh new com-mitment within twenty minutes of making it. She began to talk about something she was sad about, and Ed's Mr. Smart-Ass persona took over with a sarcastic comment. We asked them to pause, take a few breaths, and recommit.

"Would you recommit to speaking about your emotions and listening generously when the other's speaking?"

Ed sighed and looked defeated. "This is going to be hard work," he said.

"Indeed," we said. "Hardly anything worthwhile comes easy. But," we said, serving up an estate agent's metaphor, "do you plan to sell the house you live in?"

"What?" he asked.

"Are you planning to sell your own house anytime soon?"

"No," he said.

"Well, if you don't plan to sell your house, wouldn't it be better to improve it a little each day rather than chip away at the tile or spit on the floor? Even if it took a little work?"

He got the point.

RADICAL RESPONSIBILITY

So, how did we end our own cycles of blame and criticism? Here's the short answer: Every time we were conscious enough to catch ourselves uttering a critical or blameful word, we would stop (often in midsentence!) and replace it with what we came to call radical responsibility.

Radical responsibility is when you claim responsibility for something for no apparent reason, just to make good on your commitment to doing so. It's especially effective when it really looks like it's the other person's fault.

Radical responsibility is going from "How did you manage to remember the mustard and forget to buy the mayonnaise?" to "I wonder why I didn't get mayonnaise last time *I* was at the store?" Radical responsibility is shifting from saying to one of our teenagers, "I've told you three times to clean up that room and it's still an awful mess" to "I need to find a more effective way to get you to clean up your room." Blame is always about "you." Radical responsibility brings in the "I." The difference is profound.

At this point, when we're giving a public talk, a few dozen hands will shoot up in the audience with the same question: What if it actually is the other person's fault? Often someone will come up with a complete distortion of what we're talking about, something like, "You mean I'm to blame for getting my car stolen?" Questions like this illustrate the depths of misunderstanding embedded in the human mind about the simple issue of responsibility. We understand those questions because we had to clear up the same distortions in our own thinking in order to end blame and criticism in our relationship. The short answers to those questions are that even if something is one person's fault exclusively, the problem will never be resolved until the other person takes responsibility for inviting it into his or her life.

And, of course we don't think it's your fault the guy stole your car. Radical responsibility has nothing to do with blame and fault, and it can never be assigned, only taken voluntarily. It never does any good to assign responsibility to someone else: "You're responsible for stealing my car." The legal and criminal justice systems are based on assigning responsibility and apportioning blame, and we all know how spectacularly those systems don't work.

The major misunderstanding embedded in the human mind, as we noted earlier, is the inability to distinguish blame from responsibility. It's likely that most of us, when we were growing up, were exposed to this blurring of distinction: "Okay, which one of you kids is responsible for this mess?" The intention of this question is to assign blame, not to invite responsibility. Responsibility is about the ability to respond, whereas blame is about finding who is at fault. Since most of us were probably on the receiving end of this confusion of blame and responsibility, it's understandable that we would continue to perpetrate it in our later lives.

When you begin the enlightening process of taking responsibility for your life, it's important to stop confusing blame with responsibility. Blame—either taking it or dishing it out—has no healing power in relationships. Responsibility, however, has powerful healing potential. For example, if I've been blaming you for some event that happened, and suddenly I take responsibility for having cocreated it with you, both of us have the potential for a completely new relationship. You may or may not rise to the occasion by taking responsibility with me for having created the event, however; whether you do so is outside my control. In our real-life counseling situations, though, the other person often rises to the occasion, inspired by the first person's taking responsibility. This is not always the case, however. Sometimes the other person just says, "Hah! I'm glad you finally realized it's all your fault." In such a case, the only one who gets to experience liberation from the cycle of blame and criticism is the first person who claimed responsibility.

It should be noted that genuine responsibility cannot be faked. In other words, it is not possible to say sincerely that you take responsibility while secretly harboring blame. In our counseling sessions, "faked" responsibility is as obvious as a phony smile or a "thank you" that's dripping with sarcasm.

From practical experience with thousands of couples, we can tell you this: Only positive results come from one person having the courage to take responsibility. While in real life it's almost always one person who initiates taking responsibility, the real magic in relationships occurs when both people can do it together. When both people become skilled at taking responsibility, they don't waste precious time and energy in their relationship on blame. The time and energy previously consumed by blaming each other can be channeled into creative activities and intimacy.

The *Lasting Love* program restores passion and vitality quickly because it shows you how to end blame and criticism. Our experience has shown us that chronic blame signals doom for the relationship. It must be interrupted as soon as possible. According to marriage researcher John Gottman, chronic blame is one of the "Four Horsemen of the Apocalypse" (along with defensiveness, stonewalling, and contempt) that predicts divorce. In the first session we have with a couple, we ask them to make a new commitment to a no-blame relationship.

On the positive side, though, we can see a visible change in body language and energy the moment a couple makes the commitment to ending blame. Even before learning the techniques, the act of making the commitment creates a lightness in their faces. There is a simple reason for this: Blame consumes the very energy that could be used for creativity. The moment they commit to ending blame, they feel the possibility of a fresh new wave of creativity in themselves.

Blame and creativity are closely tied to each other. In a relationship, both partners will engage in blame to the extent that they are not fulfilling their own creative urges. Some people use alcohol or marijuana to distract themselves from the pain of failing to fulfill their creative potential. For other couples, blame is the drug of choice.

In our seminars and couples sessions we have developed and refined a powerful, simple, and friendly process for stopping blame. Let's now explore this process, so that you can end the creativity-sapping addiction to blame and criticism in your own life.

THE PROBLEM

The moment a word of blame leaves your mouth, your relationship ends and an entanglement begins. Then, the relationship can only be restored by ending blame and entering a zone of shared responsibility. Relationships can exist only between equals. Take a typical blame statement as an example: "You never listen to a word I say!" The relationship no longer exists the moment a phrase like this is uttered. In place of the relationship, an entanglement has emerged.

Blame is based on the presumption that there is a victim and a villain; it is based on inequality. The blamer is saying, "You are the cause of my problem," and is claiming to be of lesser power than the other. The moment blame leaves your mouth you have already decided you're the victim, handing over all the power to the other person. You have already assigned blame to the villain. You have pointed the finger and found the target.

The problem is that the person on the other end of the pointed finger doesn't feel like the villain. Your "blamee" never cheerfully agrees, "You know, you're right. Upon reflection, it's clear to me that I *am* actually responsible for all your pain." Never once in our years as psychotherapists have we ever heard anyone say anything remotely like that. What the blamee always does instead is to make a mad dash for the victim position.

You then have two people fighting for the victim position, each thinking the other is the villain. It's like a dog chasing its own tail. It produces a lot of heat and burns up a lot of energy, but it doesn't produce any positive results. The fuel consumed by the race for the victim position is the very fuel of creativity.

Therein lies the addictive power of blame: It is used in relationships as a drug to avoid the pain of not expressing creative potential.

Blame is a powerful addiction. The act of blaming another person triggers a burst of adrenalin. In its extreme form, this is the fuel for old-fashioned customs like stoning and lynching. In smaller doses, it keeps couples occupied so that they won't have to face the truly scary process of tapping into and expressing their creativity.

Notice the sensations in your body the next time you're blaming or criticizing someone. If you tune in sensitively you'll probably notice an edgy feeling of excitement and anger combined with considerable muscle tension. At a more extreme level you may notice a feeling of glee, especially if you sense you're winning the power struggle at the moment.

This very feeling—a stew of excitement, anger, tension, and glee—is the heroin and cocaine of intimate relationships. In our early attempts to end blame and criticism in our own relationship, we came to have a grudging respect for just how powerful that addictive substance is. If you're not convinced that blame and criticism are addictive, try going a full day without either one. Most people who've tried this experiment tell us they didn't manage to go even an hour before some sort of zinger left their mouths.

From the positive view, though, the fact that the couple is addicted to blame also means that they both have a wellspring of creativity trying to push through the paved-over surface of the relationship. If blame can be ended and the wellspring tapped, there are no upper limits to how much new creative juice can pour through the relationship.

What drives this addiction? In programs that treat addictions to alcohol and drugs, counselors often say that when you stop the addiction, you have to face the feelings that you originally tried to avoid by drinking or taking drugs. That's what happened to us when we stopped criticizing and blaming. As we began to get control over our tendency to blame and criticize, we noticed a fear that kept coming up over and over. To understand this fear, first look at the tendency to blame and criticize yourself.

Many of us can't go a minute, let alone an hour or a day, without critical self-talk buzzing through our minds like a squadron of mosquitoes. These nagging thoughts even go on in our sleep. How many times during the day and night do we hear thoughts such as:

• Why did I have to go and do . . . ?

• Was it a mistake to . . . ?

• I wish I hadn't . . .

• Why didn't I . . . ?

• Shouldn't I have . . . ?

Psychologists estimate that the average person cranks out fifty thousand thoughts a day. No telling how many have a critical edge to them, but some days it feels like the "mosquito thoughts" are in the majority.

Critical thoughts are all based on the fear that without them we wouldn't improve, grow, and change. That same fear drives the criticism and blame that we aim at others. We fear that without our criticism and blame, other people won't improve, grow, and change. We have high goals for ourselves and our loved ones, and we fear that without a constant barrage of criticism and blame we would all languish in mud puddles of sloth.

Blame is driven by another fear. We aim chronic blame at loved ones because we're afraid they won't take responsibility for their lives. We know intuitively that unless they seize control of their inner steering wheel, they'll not only wander aimlessly along life's freeway, they'll bash disastrously into the lives of others. But blame often has the opposite effect of the one we're seeking. When we blame another person we are trying to get them to take responsibility for something they're unwilling to own. The very act of blaming, however, disowns responsibility. Using blame to get someone to take responsibility defeats its own purpose.

We found to our great delight that we did just fine without criticism or blame. In fact, growth and change came effortlessly as we let go of our habit of criticizing. Far from dissolving into puddles of sloth, we found ourselves excited about life and growth and creativity. By not wasting energy on blame and criticism, we had more creative juice to spend as we chose. The process didn't happen overnight. It took us a few years to get to the point where we could go days and weeks without blame and criticism. Each tiny improvement along the way brought immediate rewards in the form of more harmony and creative energy. We found that slow, steady efforts to drop blame and criticism brought slow, steady growth in good feeling between us.

What if one of us had a beef with the other? What if there was some irritating behavior one of us wanted the other to change? We dealt with those kinds of things all the time—we just didn't use blame and criticism to deal with them. Dropping

blame and criticism doesn't mean you have to overlook anything, in a Pollyanna sense. For example, criticism was one of
the issues we faced in the early days of our relationship. Initially,
both of us thought we were the victims of the other person's
criticism. Gay blamed Kathlyn for being hypercritical, while
Kathlyn felt Gay was the hypercritical one. After a year or so of
wrangling about it, we finally woke up to the magic of taking
responsibility for criticism. We both decided to stop blaming
and start wondering, "Hmmm, why would I be struggling with
the issue of criticism in my life?"

Two powerful discoveries came out of our mutual wondering. The first was that we both had grown up with so much
criticism around us that we were hypervigilant for anything that
sounded remotely critical. In other words, we heard criticism
where none was actually intended. Second, we found that the
amount of intended criticism dropped dramatically because we
were no longer focused on proving that everything was the
other person's fault. Critical comments gradually became fewer
and fewer until they disappeared entirely. As of this writing, neither of us can recall a critical word of any kind in many years.

We found that it was not only possible, but relatively easy to
bring something to the other's attention in a way that wasn't
blameful or critical. In the Action Plan that follows we share the
technique of just how to do this. Does all of what we've described sound like a possibility in your life? Whether it sounds
possible or far-fetched, there's only one way to find out if it's
real. Begin as we did: with a sincere commitment to end blame
and criticism in your close relationships. We've shown several
thousand couples how to take this courageous step, and not one
of them has ever told us it wasn't worth it.

Your Action Plan

Your Commitment

"I commit to generating wonder rather than blame in all my interactions."

Your Ongoing Practice

This practice creates a blame-free zone in which appreciation and wonder flourish.

Think of blame as, "Why are you doing this to me?" and wonder as, "Hmmm, I wonder why this would be happening to me right now?" Let yourself use your whole body to practice these skills to make use of your organic body wisdom.

Take a recurring issue in your relationship and think about it for a moment. Here's the important act—notice your body posture as you think about this issue. For example, you may be slumped, or your jaw may lock up. Now do something that may seem counterproductive—exaggerate your posture for a moment to feel how the posture supports blame. As you play with exaggerating, you may be amazed to discover that it's impossible to blame unless your body posture (and more shallow breath) frames that attitude physically.

Radical responsibility springs from shifting your body attitude. Then your thinking naturally changes, too. So, after exaggerating your recurring-issue posture, make a radical change in your posture. Focus especially on opening your posture in some way. As you do that, take some relaxed belly breaths that create a sense of flow in your body.

When you have changed your posture and are breathing more freely, select one question from the following list and wonder about it through five connected breaths.

- What is familiar about my feelings, actions, and responses with this issue?
- What are my body sensations as I think of this issue?
- What can I learn from this whole issue, and what simple action step can I take that applies my learning?
- If this issue were totally resolved, what would I be doing with all that energy?

Your Ten-Second Technique

This technique generates wonder in which new possibilities emerge and problems can be resolved with ease.

First, create a pleasurable "hmmm" tone that lasts through your entire out breath. Explore different pitches and different places in your chest and throat to create your best-feeling hum.

Then, while humming, use your arm to make a big circling gesture to your heart as if you were tracing the outside of a wheel. Circle and hum two or three times while wondering: "What can I learn from this?"

If you're still in need of help

not assigning blame and working

through your issue, turn to page 226.

CHAPTER 5

The Fourth Secret

A New Kind of Creativity

Here's what creativity looks like in a *Lasting Love* relationship:

Both people are committed to exploring their own individual creative paths. At the same time, each person is committed to supporting the other partner's full creative expression. You are devoted to your own creative flourishing and the simultaneous flourishing of your partner's creativity. You don't waste your time and burn up your creative energy in repetitive power struggles. You rechannel the energy you used to waste in power struggles into deeper creative exploration. You communicate in ways that produce harmony and

passion so that the relationship itself becomes an ongoing catalyst for the full expression of both partners' creativity.

If that kind of relationship seems magical and impossible
from where you are now, you're in good company. We were a
long way from there, too, when we caught the first glimmer of
possibility. We learned, though, that it's just a matter of practicing a few essential skills over time. It's done by taking easy,
small steps that are simultaneously great leaps.

The bottom line is this: Creativity is vital to long-term relationships. Without the flow of creativity nurturing the
lifeblood of the relationship, the energy level of both people
ebbs over time. Remarkably, though, even a tiny movement toward enhanced creativity can pump new life into long-term relationships. You owe it to yourself to understand how creativity
works in relationships and what it can do for you.

THE FIRST THING TO KNOW

Here's the first thing everybody needs to know about creativity:
If both people in a relationship, you and your partner, are not
acting on your creative commitments to yourselves, you will
create relationship conflict to distract yourselves from the creative potential that's languishing inside you. Your energy level
will drop if you are not being true to your own creative urges.
Eventually you will feel dull and dissatisfied.

That's only part of the problem, though. The bigger
problem is that when people feel dull and dissatisfied, they tend
to blame the relationship for the problem. They think the relationship is the source of the boredom and dissatisfaction, rather

than the unfulfilled inner commitment to creativity. Then, each person tries to get the partner to change so that the boredom will be replaced by liveliness. These dramas are resolved only when each of you takes responsibility for finding the source of creativity inside yourself. The partnership flourishes as each of you takes steps toward expressing that creativity.

Creativity Is Infinite

The biggest barrier we run up against in counseling couples about their creativity is simply this: People don't think they're creative. They have defined creativity too narrowly—they don't think it's within their power to be creative. They associate creativity only with traditional artistic expressions such as painting, dance, and music. If you've fallen into this trap, it's critical for you to understand that creativity has infinite expressions. The art of resolving the creativity problems in a relationship lies in each person's discovery of his or her own tools. For one person it can mean 10 minutes of spontaneous wild dance every day. For another person it is a cup of tea and a half hour of solitude.

What Creativity Is

Our definition of creativity comes from practical experience in helping couples revitalize their relationships. In other words, we base our definition purely on what has worked to bring passion and productivity back into long-term relationships. This experience brought us to a very different understanding of creativity: *Creativity is anything that takes you out of the zone of the known and into the zone of wonder.* In order to bring vitality to relationships, people need to spend a little time, preferably every day, in a state of wonder and invention. Whatever it takes to do that is your best form of creativity.

By this definition, practically anything can be creative. Making soup is just as creative an activity as writing a novel, as long as it contains a teaspoon of invention and a dash of wonder. Even if you've made the same soup every day for 30 years, you can turn it into a creative experience with a moment of wonder: "Hmmm, I wonder how it would be if I added a sprig or two of basil?" Wonder and invention are sure cures for boredom and dissatisfaction. Staying within the zone of the known drains energy and saps satisfaction.

The Power of Creativity

Creativity has awesome power. If we nurture our creativity it can literally save our lives; if we squelch it we lose the vital wellspring that makes us feel really alive. One thing we've learned from our own lives, as well as from working with other couples, is that one of the greatest sources of pain in the world is unfulfilled creative potential. On the positive side, though, it only takes a small opening to creativity for it to produce a major rebirth in the vitality of a relationship.

A MAJOR REALIZATION

We'd like to go into more depth about a point we touched on earlier. If you understand it, you can save a great deal of stress and agony in relationships.

When people aren't expressing their own creative potential, they focus blame on the relationship. Another way to say it: When you find yourself complaining about your relationship, the problem you're complaining about is usually not the real problem. The real problem is that you aren't opening up to your own personal creativity. Of the 3,000 or so couples we've worked with, about 2,990 of them didn't understand this point. We didn't understand it, either, when we first got together. We had to figure it out "the hard way" because it's not something we were ever taught in school. Not even in our master's and doctoral programs! We think it's so important that it ought to be part of the curriculum from kindergarten on up.

We're not saying that people are hallucinating the relationship problems they're complaining about. Usually, when a person points a finger at something in the relationship that's going wrong, the finger is aimed at something real—*it's just aimed at that reality prematurely.* For example, if you blame your spouse for sabotaging the relationship by drinking too much alcohol, chances are there is some reality to your complaint. The first place to deal with the problem, however, is by opening up more to your own creativity, rather than aiming more criticism at your spouse. Your concern with your spouse's bad habits may be a smokescreen to cover your own dissatisfaction with how little of your creative potential you're expressing. Your spouse may be doing the very same thing, but using the smokescreen of alcohol. Rather than trying to change your spouse's behavior, go into a room by yourself and use that energy to write a poem (if writing is your creative path). When you come out, after having expressed your creative potential, you may find that your spouse has been inspired to follow your example.

There's even a foolproof "acid test" we've developed through our work with couples. Here's how to know beyond a shadow of a doubt that the real problem is your unexpressed creativity: If you've complained about something in another person three or more times and it hasn't changed, you can be sure the problem needs to be addressed inside yourself.

The first task is to stop complaining and address the problem by focusing on your own creativity. If you're in touch with your creativity, your attention to things you want to change has a greater chance of producing positive results. The reason: Your living commitment to your creativity brings authority to your focus. In addition, an increased commitment to creativity by one person often has an inspirational effect on the other person in the relationship.

If you're out of touch with your creativity, you will keep complaining about things and they won't ever change. The complaining has become a distraction to keep your attention away from the real issue: unexpressed creative potential.

Here's the principle again: If there is an ongoing complaint or series of complaints in a relationship, look first to the creative potential that's not being expressed. When you don't open up to your creative impulses, you take it out on the relationship. Let's use a real-life example to explore the principle in depth.

WE WORKED with a couple we'll call Patrick and Chris who had been together fifteen years, and married for the last ten of those years. In our first session with them, Chris said that her major complaint was that "he's never here." What she meant was that he spent a lot of time at work, and even when he was at home his mind seemed somewhere else.

Patrick's complaint was that Chris was "relentlessly critical." He spent a lot of time at work, he said, because the moment he came through the front door of their house she started criticizing him for one thing and another. He said, "Even when I'm here she criticizes me for not being here."

It was a classic set of complaints, well worn into the fabric of their relationship like a set of deep grooves across the living room carpet. They'd obviously been through the complaints many times, and we'd heard hundreds of couples say something very similar.

It's a human tendency to think that one's complaints are unique. It's an even more powerful human tendency to think one's complaints are real and valid. It came as a surprise to this couple when we told them that we'd heard many other couples voice the same general complaint. They were more than surprised, however, when we asked them if they'd be willing to get to the real source of those complaints within themselves. They got mad. At us.

CHRIS: Are you trying to tell me he doesn't spend too much time thinking about work?

PATRICK: So you think I'm making it up that she criticizes me all the time?

We invited them to take a deep breath and love themselves for getting defensive. We told them that getting defensive is a perfectly good thing—it lets us know we're on the right track.

One of the first things good therapists learn in their training is the Law of Defensive Reactions: When you or your client gets defensive, you know you've uncovered something crucial. When you see a classic defensive reaction (think of Bill Clinton wagging a finger and denying allegations of sexual misconduct), you know there's something just under the surface that the person is desperately trying to hide. It also means there's something just under the surface that the person desperately wants to reveal. The war between wanting to hide it and wanting to reveal it produces the defensive reaction.

IN THE CASE of Patrick and Chris, they were both trying to hide their deep dissatisfaction with their own creative potential. Each of them had sold themselves out in the creativity department—he wanted to stay at home, she wanted to work—and they couldn't stand facing that they had done so. As a result, they took their anger out on the relationship by blaming the other person. To avoid facing the inner despair of unexpressed creativity, they focused on the faults and flaws of each other. Each of them was convinced that if only the other person would change, life would be much better.

To make matters worse, all their friends agreed. His friends agreed that it was all her fault; her friends were unanimous in blaming him for the unhappiness in the marriage. This issue points to a difficult barrier that makes personal change even more challenging than it already is. Not only do we lock into the habit of complaining about the other person, we get our friends to agree that those complaints are real and justified. We bolster our perception of reality by getting our friends to vote for its validity.

That's how this particular couple had entrenched themselves in a cycle of complaint that had drained the energy from their once vibrant marriage.

Just beneath the surface, however, is where the real issues and ulti-mate salvation of the relationship can be found. Some wise person once said, "You're never upset for the reason you think you are," and this couple was a living example of the truth of that saying. When they had the courage to dive beneath the surface of their complaints, they brought the vitality back to their relationship in a remarkably short period of time.

The real problem was in the zone of creativity, and it had started when their first child was born. When they were first married, she was a successful lawyer and he was rising quickly through the executive ranks in a software corporation.

After they were married they began a family right away. At this point Chris put work on the back burner. In fact, she quit her job to stay at home with the two children they eventually had. Now, though, the children were in school most of the day. She hungered to get back into the world of work. She mentioned that she had started to write an article for a law journal while she was pregnant with her first child. Now, her second child was in kindergarten and she had yet to finish writing the article.

As we worked with her, it became clear that she was angry and envious of Patrick's passion for his career. Inside, she felt she had lost any chance she ever had of career success. So naturally, when he came in the door full of workday buzz, her anger and jealousy kicked in and she turned, as she put it, into a "bitching machine."

Under the surface Patrick was angry with her for being able to stay home. After twenty years of pushing to get ahead at work, he had secretly built up a backload of envy for a life without push. He found himself fantasizing about chucking his career and taking the family to live on a sheep ranch in the outback of Australia.

His other big complaint was that she was boring. According to him, she had put all her energy into supporting him and raising kids and had neglected the process of keeping her mind alive. He wanted a cocreative partner, not just a supportive partner.

Getting Them to Change

Making the commitment to change is the hardest part of any change process.

It took the better part of three one-hour sessions with Patrick and Chris to get to the point at which they both could say honestly, "Yes, I commit to making the changes necessary to revitalize our relationship." A sludgy sense of inertia settles around people when they have been stuck for a long time so that the very idea of making a change seems too daunting a task.

In addition, both of them had various degrees of resistance to tapping their own creative wellspring. Their resistance took the shape and form we'd seen in hundreds of other couples.

BARRIERS TO CREATIVITY

Most barriers to creativity are based on fears that need to be explored and laid to rest. Let's begin with perhaps the most common barrier. Chris summed up the first barrier very succinctly: "I don't know what creativity is, but whatever it is, I'm not." She had always thought of herself as a "doer" and "the tortoise instead of the hare," and she had never felt an authentic connection with her inner creative source.

The Barrier of Intimacy

Both of them shared a second barrier: I can't be creative as an individual and be in a close relationship, too. Religious programming played a role for him in this barrier. He had been brought up in a family where several members were nuns and priests. In his mind he had made a division between spiritual growth and marriage: You couldn't be married and also be deeply committed to your own spiritual development.

This barrier presents an obstacle for many people. Few role models show us that it's possible to embrace our creative genius and be in an intimate relationship at the same time. There are plenty of examples of people who turned their backs on intimacy in order to open up a pipeline to their creative genius. Henry David Thoreau didn't take Mrs. Thoreau to Walden Pond with him (not that he had a missus, anyway). Albert Einstein managed to write an entire autobiography without remembering to mention his first wife and their children. The poet Rainer Maria Rilke wouldn't come downstairs for his daughter's wedding because he was working on a poem and didn't want to break his concentration. Where are the famous examples of people who've opened up to their full capacity for both intimacy and creativity?

We've worked with many couples who've faced this barrier: If I open up to my creativity, it will take me away from my relationships. This barrier is based on the split many of us feel between love and creativity. Most of us have seen examples of the "lone genius" who must withdraw from life and love in order to express his or her gifts. This type of programming leaves us with the impression that we will need to renounce the world of home and family to go wherever our genius takes us. We fear we must sacrifice the comforts of home in order to soar to our creative heights, and this fear clips our creative wings. We sacrifice our creativity and stay home, but instead of enjoying its comforts we chafe at the cage it becomes.

The Barrier of Roles

Within the barrier of intimacy is embedded another fear: If I open up to my creativity, even a little bit, I'll shake up the roles and comfort level of the relationship. Here's an extreme example:

A WOMAN COMPLAINED that her husband controlled her every move. "Even if I go down to the grocery store for a half hour, he's on the cell phone reminding me to get something he's already told me to get at least three times!"

On the spot we hatched a radical "therapy" technique: a solo walk around the block. We asked them to take a fifteen-minute walk, each choosing his or her separate creative path. "Just go for a walk by yourself, paying no attention to where the other person chooses to go. Then come back in fifteen minutes and tell us what happened."

The fifteen minutes of being left to their own creative devices proved to be a revelation for both of them. When they returned they were bright-eyed and full of energy, but the journey had been anything but easy. Along the way they encountered in miniature just about every barrier we're describing here.

He told us he spent the first five minutes of the walk obsessing about where she was. Then he started wondering if she would still love him if he truly started doing things on his own without her.

Meanwhile, his wife was running her version of the drama. "I actually started feeling nauseous in my stomach about halfway up the block. I had to look back over my shoulder to make sure he was doing it right. The wave of fear I felt in my stomach really shook me up. How could something as simple as going for a walk around the block by myself make me scared? I realized that I'd been thinking for ten years that he was the control freak in the family, but I had to face the facts—I'm just as big a control freak as he is."

Their control struggles were all based on *fear*. In their individual ways, they were scared that if they opened up to their creativity, they would lose the relationship.

The Barrier of Time

Time is often a third barrier for many people. Most people simply don't think they have enough time to express their creative genius and handle all their real-world responsibilities, too. We faced this issue ourselves early in our relationship. The resolution of it gave us a huge growth spurt in our individual creativity as well as an increase in the flow of love between us.

It wasn't easy, though. When we got together, Gay took on the role of the "creative" one, while Kathlyn fell into the role of the "supportive" one. One problem was that we were both good at our respective roles. The bigger problem was that both of us had outgrown those roles but didn't know quite how to get out of them.

KATHLYN: I'd been brought up to be "Mom's helper" in a family with two brothers and a father who needed a lot of maintenance. One of my earliest memories is of my mother showing me how to operate the buttons on the washing machine. In adult life, I'd fallen into the role of being "the good woman behind the great man," and although I was unconsciously chafing to break out into the spotlight myself, I felt restricted by the pull of my old "helper" role.

GAY: I was already well known by the time I met Katie, due to the success of some of my early books. It was very easy for me to occupy the role of the "star" in my relationship with her because she was so incredibly good at handling all the domestic and social responsibilities that I didn't like to handle.

KATHLYN: One of the big breakthroughs came when Gay pointed out to me how I organized my time. One day I was complaining to him that I had to do all the dishes and put in a load of wash before I could sit down to work on my doctoral dissertation. I think I was also slipping in a jab at him for sitting there happily typing away on his new book while I was occupied with drudgery. He said, "You know, you don't actually have to do the dishes first. You could put your creative activities as a higher priority than your chores."

Although it sounds so simple and obvious, it was like a light bulb turning on in my mind. Suddenly I saw how I'd imposed an unnecessary rule on myself: Do the chores before you do anything you want to do yourself. I realized I could easily put my creativity first. Gay then threw in the clincher by saying, "Why don't you try it out? While you're working on your dissertation, I'll take a break from my writing and do the dishes and laundry."

GAY: I realized that I knew a lot about being the "creative one" in a relationship, but I didn't know anything about being in a relationship with a woman who was expressing her own creativity to the maximum. Was it even possible? Who would do the dishes?

KATHLYN: I put myself on a strict "creativity first" program. I got up every day and did my creative work before I handled any domestic chores, even the ones I really liked such as cooking. It was tough. Practically every day I felt the pull of my old programming telling me to do the "dirty work" first. It took a lot of discipline for several months to get myself in the habit of putting my creative activities first.

The remarkable discovery for both of us was that all the domestic stuff got done just fine. We still washed the dishes, did the laundry, and paid the bills—we just did it all after we finished the creative work. It probably took us less time since the chores were being done by two happy people. The thing that most couples don't realize is that the creative commitment frees up energy that suddenly makes things possible that haven't happened before.

The Barrier of Failure

There's another barrier that many of us must face when we open up to our creativity: What if we actually express our creative potential fully and it fails? That fear probably causes many of us to keep our creative urges thoroughly squelched. Our unconscious mind thinks, "Better to live a dull life with hidden potential than express that potential and be laughed at or ignored." Many people create an artificial barrier by thinking that their creativity must be hitched to commercial success. In their minds, creativity must produce results in the marketplace in order to be considered successful. Some even set an impossibly high bar to jump over to get to their creativity. They think, "I've got to do it perfectly or not at all." Inevitably this way of thinking leads to despair: Since few of us are Mozart, why bother trying to express our creativity on the piano? This way of thinking, however, misses the main point of creative expression: It's the flow of creativity itself that's important, not the commercial result. Most creativity doesn't generate cash or glory—it generates a feeling of inner satisfaction and aliveness. When you're in the darkness at night, waiting to go to sleep, that feeling of satisfaction is what really matters. In those quiet moments when we're alone with ourselves, we're not counting cash or headlines. . . . We're tuning in to whether we've kept our inner creative fires glowing brightly that day. As an inspiration, watch children at play. They're immersed in enjoyment of the activity for its own sake, regardless of any anticipated reward.

An important component in tapping your creativity is the courage it takes to put yourself in situations where you don't know what's coming next. Creativity takes us into a zone in which we're actively engaged in wondering and learning something new in each moment.

YOUR GENIUS

Most of us don't realize it, but we're harboring a genius inside us. Ultimately, a Lasting Love relationship is about the liberation of that inner genius. Our inner genius wants very much to be expressed. If you will liberate your genius and give it a voice, before you know it you'll be feeling more vibrant energy than you ever imagined. Your close relationships will directly benefit from your decision to open up to your genius.

How do you liberate your inner genius? First, think of every person as having four zones:

GENIUS
EXCELLENCE
COMPETENCE
INCOMPETENCE

Let's start with incompetence because it's easy to think of things we're not good at. In your zone of incompetence are all those things that almost anyone can do better than you can. For example, one of us (Gay) is pathetically incompetent at mechanical devices of all kinds. Put a screwdriver in his hand and he becomes a danger to any mechanical object he touches. Kathlyn, on the other hand, is excellent at fixing mechanical things. She comes from a family in which her father and her two brothers are engineers. The ability to fix things is part of the family tradition. You can find out your areas of incompetence by asking what you spend a lot of time doing that your partner and friends can all do better and with greater ease.

In your zone of competence are the things you can do fairly well, but others can do them just as well. You may be competent at doing the laundry or balancing your bank account, but it's likely that someone else could do it about as well.

In your zone of excellence are those things you can do better than most people. You might be an excellent golfer or an excellent cook. You get feedback that other people look up to your abilities in that area.

Your genius zone contains your gifts and unique abilities. You know you're in your zone of genius when you're doing things you love. You lose your sense of time when you're in your genius zone, and you can stay there for hours without getting tired. If you work in an organization, your genius is that skill or quality nobody else brings to the table. If it were missing, the organization would miss it.

Most people don't realize, however, that excellence can bog them down and become a trap. You might have learned to do something better than most of the people around you and have been rewarded for that skill. Kathlyn, for example, can organize just about anything better than most chief executive officers of major companies. She has been paid well to organize and has received lots of attention for these skills. Though ordering, sorting, and compiling gives her satisfaction, it does not make Kathlyn's heart sing, nor is it unique. When you're expressing your genius, you'll feel vibrantly alive.

Our experience in working with couples has shown us that people spend far too much time in their zones of incompetence and competence, and far too little time in their zones of excellence and genius. They get bogged down in doing a lot of things that others could do as well or better, so they squander the time and energy they could be spending in their zones of excellence and genius.

We all need to face ourselves squarely and ask: How much time do we spend in our zone of genius? An even bolder question is: How much time do we waste in our zones of incompetence and competence?

Many people don't even allow these questions to surface because they get trapped in the common problems that inhibit genius. See if any of these issues are familiar:

1. You haven't identified your genius.

2. You don't prioritize your time and energy to feed your genius.

3. You get entranced by complaining about your incompetence and feel victimized by it.

4. You keep trying without success to become competent at something that has resided in your incompetent zone for some time.

5. You don't know how to delegate.

6. You don't know how to say "no."

Numbers three through six are what we call dramas of competence and incompetence. They are very popular because they keep people from allowing fears of the unknown and fears of success to emerge. You can engage others fairly easily in "ain't it awful" conversations that confirm your worst visions of yourself and your possibilities. It's much more uncommon to find people avidly discussing their unique contributions and the activities they love. We recommend dealing with your incompetent and competent areas with three moves. First, see if these areas can be delegated. It's actually possible that your area of incompetence is someone else's genius.

Here's an example of the costs of not delegating and the freedom that results from placing attention on genius and excellence. Pete, a friend of ours, told us about spending thirteen hours one Saturday installing and debugging a new printer. He told us about it in detail because we had recommended that particular printer to him. Four of those hours were spent "on hold" waiting to speak to the technical support staff about problems that came up during the installation. The experience was maddeningly frustrating, and based on our discussion of the four zones, it's easy to see why. He took on a project that was, at best, in his zone of competence.

These choices can be costly both in money and in energy that could be spent in more creative activities. When Pete is doing his consulting work, where he's in his zones of excellence and genius, he bills his time at £250 an hour. In purely financial terms, he spent the equivalent of £3,250 installing the printer. By contrast, because we know we're inept at such things, we hired an expert for £65 an hour to install ours. He had the printer and a few other items installed within four hours. He left happily with his check for £260, and we were left with our sanity intact. Pete was still upset about his experience several days later, so the toll on his creative energy probably cost him a few more thousands.

The second and third radical moves in your incompetent and competent areas are related. Can you avoid this incompetent skill by seeing it coming and getting out of the way? For example, when people begin a conversation with Gay about anything mechanical, he cheerfully admits his incompetence and starts talking about something he feels passionate about.

Can you get rid of this area altogether so you never have to discuss it again? For example, in a couples' course about a year ago, a woman realized that she despised doing laundry. She had struggled with the chore out of a sense of duty for many years but still managed to mix up the whites and shrink her husband's favorite shirts. They had a truthful conversation in front of the group in which the husband then confessed that he really liked to do laundry and considered himself quite a connoisseur of the laundry world. He hadn't stepped in or spoken up out of fear of being criticized by his macho friends. They made an agreement that henceforth in their marriage, she would not even have to consider the laundry. He agreed to let himself fully enjoy the tangible pleasures of clean, folded clothes and linens. We checked with them recently and found that the wife had quite happily not done laundry for over twelve months, and the husband continued to find this activity a centering aesthetic expression. And here was the pleasant surprise: She had used her liberated energy to start a whole new skin care business based on her genius skill of nurturing that provided work for both of them and financial and creative abundance.

Here are some questions that can assist you in evoking genius:

- What is my genius, and how can I bring it forth so that it really serves me and others in the world at the same time?

- What is it I need to do to enable me to live in my genius most of the time?

- How can I live in my genius in my closest relationships?

- How can I enjoy and express my genius all the time?

- Am I willing to prosper by acting from my genius all the time?

With these questions in mind, let's form a plan to make a living commitment to creativity in the real world of your daily activities. Turn the page for your Action Plan.

Your Action Plan

Your Commitment

"I commit to the full experience and expression of my creativity, and I commit to supporting my partner's full creativity."

Your Ongoing Practice

Take five to ten minutes a day for your creative practice. Make this time a creative calisthenics workout. You'll be developing your creative muscles. The nature of this practice stretches your beliefs about what you can do, what your limitations and possibilities are, and how creative you can be. It's important for this time to be nonproductive in the literal sense. It is not intended to produce a product or anything that anyone else could judge as useful or valuable. It is intended to bring you directly into your creative flow. Schedule this time with whatever method you normally use for organizing, for example, a Palm Pilot or wall calendar. Most people find that if they put their creativity first, that is, make it their first daily priority, the rest of the day flows with greater joy. If you wait until you've completed your work, your household responsibilities, your child care, etc., the wellspring dries up. You may be surprised to find out how little real time is necessary to renew and develop your genuine creativity if you do it first.

What could you use to practice your creativity? Here are some possibilities: You could use art materials to make collages or finger paint. You might put on your favorite music and let your body move. You could combine making unusual sounds and using your nondominant hand to write. Go into the kitchen and make something using ingredients that never go together. Open a journal and write down whatever words pop into your mind. Choose something you love to experience that you don't usually find time for during the busy day.

Notice that we are not suggesting that you compose a symphony, write a poem, or complete that novel. The creative practice is just that: practice. You are learning to listen to your own creative voice and to cultivate its expression.

Your Ten-Second Technique

Catch yourself in a routine in your relationship. For example, notice if you always walk on one side of your partner. If so, walk on the other side for a week or two. If one of you usually initiates sex, have the other one initiate for a while. If one of you is the "talker," change roles for a week. Whatever the routine is, change it.

CHAPTER 6

The Fifth Secret

Tandem Acts of Kindness

In our first year together, we spent quite a bit of time thinking and talking about the kind of relationship we wanted to create. We were both keenly committed to inventing a relationship that was different from anything we'd experienced as adults, as well as what we'd seen around us growing up. We tried to make a list of role models, people whose relationships we admired or thought we could learn from. After evaluating twenty or so couples who had long-term relationships that seemed to work fairly well, we concluded that none of them really were doing anything we wanted to emulate. So, we decided it was going to have to be a do-it-yourself project.

Sitting in front of the fireplace in our house, we hit upon a strategy for creating a new kind of relationship with each other. We made a list of all the things we wished would have been part of past relationships. On the list were things like *emotional availability* and *feeling appreciated*. Then, we began to invent a way of being with each other that made those things a part of our relationship. One thing we began to do was to express verbal appreciations to each other. We had never seen anybody do anything like that in our families of origin, nor had we thought to do it in past relationships of our own.

It worked sensationally well! Just remembering to speak simple appreciations to each other throughout the day had an almost magical effect on the feeling of harmony in our relationship. Each time we would say, "I appreciate you for making breakfast this morning," or, "Thanks for doing such a great job teaching the workshop tonight," we would feel an upsurge of positive energy between us. Soon it became an ongoing part of our relationship, to the extent that we did it absentmindedly.

One such moment sticks in our memories. We were invited to go to the movies with another couple who had been together about the same length of time. On the way in the car, Gay spoke a verbal appreciation to Kathlyn, along the lines of "I really appreciate how beautiful you look tonight." The two heads in the front seat whipped around in unison to look at us. The man said, somewhat jokingly, "That's it? You're just going to appreciate her for no reason?" His mate said, also jokingly but with a slight edge of envy, "What's so wrong with that?" "Nothing," he said. "You just don't hear people say things like that out loud very often."

That was the way it was back then, but in the years since we've done everything we could to change that condition. During the past twenty-plus years we've had the pleasure of helping many couples learn how to appreciate each other more skillfully. Through this experience we've gained deep respect for the power of appreciation to change lives. Although appreciation is a simple process, most of us are so rusty that it's often a challenge—even for couples who are committed to learning. Once they get the hang of it, though, they find it to be an essential part of their relationship.

A COURAGEOUS CHOICE

When you make the commitment to learn the skill of appreciating, you're making a choice that's not only powerful—it's courageous to the point of being radical. When you choose to live your life from a space of appreciation, you break free of a repetitive rut that most of humanity lives in.

Here's what we mean.

If you look and listen as you go through your day, you'll soon realize that all of us live in one of two ongoing cycles: a cycle of appreciation or a cycle of entitlement and complaint, which we covered in chapter 1. As an experiment to confirm this for yourself, stop and listen for a few minutes to the conversations around you in a busy place such as a coffee shop or airport newsstand. We've done this many times, and the conversations never fail to be mainly about the subject of relationships. If you listen to the tone of those conversations, you can hear that they are coming either out of appreciation or out of entitlement and complaint. Put simply, the cycle of entitlement and complaint goes like this:

We want something from our partner. Not only do we want it, but we feel entitled to it. Of course, we don't get what we want, so we complain about it and criticize our partner. Then the situation improves temporarily, or it doesn't. Eventually we again start feeling we're not getting what we're entitled to, so we complain and criticize more.

That's the cycle of entitlement and complaint.

The cycle of appreciation is radically different and goes like this:

We make a commitment to living in a cycle of appreciation. As we go through the day we look for things to appreciate about our partner, either new things or old. We speak our appreciations clearly, and this causes us to see more things to appreciate.

THE SECRET

What most of us don't know is this: We have a choice about which cycle to live in. What most of us *really* need to know is how to get out of the cycle of complaint and into the cycle of appreciation.

First, Be Easy on Yourself

Please don't beat yourself up if you've been living in a cycle of complaint. There's really no good reason why any of us should be good at appreciating. Appreciation is an art and a science, but hardly anyone has had any training in it. At our seminars, we often begin our exploration of appreciation by asking the participants to do a quick check on themselves. You can do it now.

Think of someone you love.

Now think of something you really appreciate about that person. Get a picture or feeling of something that person does that you really appreciate. Now ask yourself: How long has it been since I spoke that appreciation sincerely and clearly to him or her?

Has it been a while? If so, you're in good company. Even the good-hearted, open-minded people who come to relationship seminars discover to their surprise that they've been extremely stingy with speaking their appreciation to the people they love.

The good news is that the art of appreciation can be learned quickly. The even better news is that when you bring that art home to the real world of your close relationships, miracles will start to appear before your very eyes.

THE RELATIONSHIP PYRAMID

Relationships are based on a pyramid of paradigms. At the bottom of the pyramid, relationships are based on a survival paradigm. In that part of the world in which more than a billion people live in poverty, partners are focused on carrying out specific roles such as provider and protector and nurturer. If you don't stay within your role, your physical survival is at stake.

If you think back to the very beginnings of your life, you can see that all of us rely on relationships for survival. From the moment of conception to well after birth, we can't survive without another person. For the first nine months of life, our mothers are the biological matrix that holds us. For a long while after birth, other people hold the power over our survival. Our original relationships are imprinted on every breath we take, so it's natural for us to carry the survival programming of early life into our relationships as adults.

The survival thrust of relationships goes on for years, with the rules being very simple: Do whatever it takes to survive.

In the middle level of the pyramid, a smaller number of people are fortunate enough to have relationships based on a fulfillment paradigm. Partners are focused less on survival and more on fulfilling career goals, self-esteem goals, or expression-of-potential goals. In the fulfillment paradigm, considerable energy is also directed toward solving problems and handling issues that emerge as barriers to each partner's fulfillment. At this level, couples can make great use of counseling and relationship seminars.

In our adult relationships, we raise the bar, remake the rules, and change the game. We enter a new world, one that has not been in existence for very long. We turn our relationships into a quest for learning and fulfillment. We yearn to feel whole inside, and we know that relationships are the key to that wholeness. Here, a crucial error in thinking is often made: We think the other person is there to complete our lack of wholeness. If we feel an inner lack of wholeness, we look to other people to make us feel whole. In reality, our partners are not there to make us complete. It's up to us to make ourselves whole, just as it's up to others to make themselves whole.

Then, two whole people can enjoy a dance of intimacy as free spirits who are playing together out of choice. The alternative is not so graceful—more like one of those three-legged races where one of each partner's legs is bound to the other.

At the top of the pyramid, a smaller number of people are discovering an exciting new paradigm. They are basing their relationships on a gratitude paradigm in which the focus is not on problem solving or fulfillment, but on the art of appreciating. Partners are focused on the moment-by-moment celebration of the other person. In the gratitude paradigm you also must survive and seek fulfillment, but your primary focus is on appreciation.

This new paradigm gives a spiritual dimension to appreciation. This dimension takes the art of appreciation beyond the practical value of enjoying more loving relationships. Learning how to give and receive appreciation is the same holy task as the larger process of opening to the flow of connection with the divine nature of the universe itself. To appreciate another person effectively, you must resonate with his or her essence—the core nature of that person at the most fundamental level of being. To receive an appreciation from another person, you must undergo a benign ego surrender and let yourself be touched on that same level of essence. Viewed from this perspective, the art of appreciating becomes a valid path for healing the breaches that divide us from ourselves, others, and the universe.

WHY LEARN THE ART
OF APPRECIATION?

Here are some of the reasons why we'd like you to get as excited about appreciation as we are.

• First, the act of appreciating another person literally works wonders: It's the fastest way we've ever seen of opening a flow of connection in a relationship. When that flow opens, all sorts of amazing transformations start to happen in the relationship. For example, appreciation has a remarkable power to solve problems. It changes the things you don't like about your partner faster than criticism, threats, sarcasm, rewards, or any other popular "motivational" tools that couples use on each other. The act of appreciating people causes them to let go of negative patterns of behavior much faster than criticizing those same behavior patterns. Specifically, skillfully appreciating an intimate partner decreases the number of things he or she does that bother you. There are two good reasons for this. First, your act of appreciating puts you in a more positive mood so you are less influenced by the other's behavior. Second, your appreciation builds the other's positive energy and self-esteem, which causes the person to engage less in the troublesome behavior.

We have data on more than four hundred cases in which a troublesome pattern of behavior (which had been resistant to criticism, sometimes for decades) changed quickly when a rich flow of appreciation was initiated. A case in point: One of our clients often criticized her husband for "leaving his stuff lying around." She had been criticizing him for this behavior throughout their twelve-year marriage, *with no effect whatsoever* on the problem behavior. He still left his stuff lying around. We asked her to declare her criticism project a failure and hang it up. In its place, we asked her to try a new program. To make matters more interesting, we asked her to change her program without telling him what she was doing.

The new program: She made an agreement with us to stop criticizing him altogether for a week. Instead, she agreed to put her energy into speaking appreciations to him. We asked her to speak one appreciation the first day, two the second day, and so on. On the fourth day, something magical happened: He straightened up the area around his side of the bed. (Remember: He knew nothing about the experiment she was conducting.) By the end of the week he was reliably picking up things he had previously left lying around.

Will this work for you? Conduct your own experiment and find out. The woman in this example initially was convinced it would never work "in a million years." Our experience taught us otherwise.

- Appreciation is a powerful healer. People enjoy better health and less illness in relationships where there's a vital flow of appreciation.

- The act of appreciating creates beauty. People become more beautiful the more they're appreciated. Your partner will get a more beautiful glow as you become more skilled at appreciating him or her.

- Appreciation has a way of looping back on itself in positive ways. The more you appreciate others, the more you appreciate yourself. Then, this deeper appreciation for yourself will give you a heightened ability to appreciate others.

- Appreciation is a priceless gift you can give to your partner any time, any place, for any reason. It costs nothing and it can be infinitely more valuable than a mansion and rubies.

- Appreciation is a mood shifter. Appreciation will get you out of a low mood or a relationship conflict quickly, no matter how long you've been stuck or trapped. Even if it doesn't produce any tangible results, appreciation is still valuable because it feels so good. The body feeling of gratitude is a delicious sensation to enjoy inside yourself.

• Appreciation is an ideal way to fill the time during periods of transition or indecision. For instance, you may be trying to decide whether to leave a relationship or stay in it. If you have no immediate plans to leave, it's wise to spend your time appreciating yourself and your partner. For example, if you were thinking of buying a new car, you would still take care of the one you have until you make your decision about the future. The same is true for relationships.

Our Discovery

When we first turned the microscope on our relationship we found that we were stingy with verbal appreciation. As we became more sensitive to appreciation and the lack of it, we saw that being stingy with appreciation is common not just in romantic relationships. We've observed it in sessions of marital therapy, family therapy, and corporate coaching. Indeed, the art of appreciating is so unfamiliar and poorly understood that most people do not think of it as something that can be learned. In our seminars it takes the average group less than four hours to move from hopelessly clumsy to amazingly capable as they learn this life-altering skill.

Our most significant discovery is that particular kinds of spoken appreciation cause rapid, positive changes in relationships. We have found other types of appreciation to be useful, but there is nothing we've found that compares to the specific techniques of verbal appreciation that we illustrate later in this chapter.

WHAT APPRECIATION IS

First, let's change the noun into a verb. While appreciation is a good thing, it's really the act of *appreciating* that produces miracles of intimacy. Here's what we mean when we talk about appreciating.

First, appreciating is the act of becoming sensitively aware of a person or thing. To appreciate is to become *conscious of details and nuances*, according to the dictionary. For example, one who appreciates art is attuned to the nuances that distinguish a drawing by DaVinci from one by Caravaggio. We'd like you to make a heartfelt commitment to becoming sensitively aware of yourself and of your mate (or anyone with whom you desire closeness). This commitment will help you begin to master the art of tuning in more closely to detail and nuance.

Second, appreciating is the act of focusing on the positive aspects of a person or object. An example: You single out a positive aspect of your partner and communicate it directly, as in, "I appreciate the way you helped Noah with his homework last night." In troubled relationships there is approximately a one-to-one ratio of positive to negative interactions, whereas in healthy relationships the ratio is greater than five to one. Appreciating changes the ratio immediately toward the positive.

Third, appreciating is the act of adding value. If you care for a house, for example, it will increase in value. Most of us want our relationships to grow in value, but few of us know the active ways to make it happen from moment to moment. Appreciating gives you a map and a powerful set of techniques for adding value in every moment.

A Point of Clarification

We want to emphasize that appreciating is not a form of Pollyanna-ish "positive thinking" employed to ignore, deny, or skip over any problems in a relationship. In fact, relationships thrive only when you acknowledge whatever emerges—even the unwelcome, the unexpected, and the highly irritating. Relationships flourish when you handle emerging issues in a straightforward fashion, as we showed in chapter 4, and then you make a conscious choice to shift into appreciation.

If you're cringing in the dental chair, gripped by the fear of the whining drill, we don't believe you should chant "I really, really appreciate this" in your mind to distract yourself. Instead, acknowledge the fear, the irritation, and the noise. Give those unpleasant elements a moment of clear attention; then switch to appreciating the positive aspects of the moment as soon as you can. You might appreciate the skill of your dentist, for example, as well as the comparison with dentistry a hundred years ago. In actual practice, the act of acknowledging the current reality—"I HATE BEING IN THIS DENTAL CHAIR RIGHT NOW!"—switches on the "appreciation machinery" automatically, provided you're committed to appreciation in general.

THE POWER OF APPRECIATION

We would like to give an example of appreciation in action, drawn from one of our relationship seminars.

A MAN AND WOMAN stood with us in front of several hundred people. It was the final afternoon of the three-day workshop, and we were beginning the module in which we teach men and women the strategies of appreciation. This long-married couple had volunteered for a ten-minute demonstration of one of our foundation techniques for expressing verbal appreciation.

First, we asked him to express an appreciation to her without any coaching by us. He stumbled a little, then spoke a rambling sentence to her: "Um, something I like . . . well, hmmm, I think you wear really nice clothes. Yeah, you always look great when we go out." When he came to a halt she gave him a slight smile of encouragement. Other than that, her expression didn't change. It was clear that his appreciation did nothing to move her, and the audience murmured and shifted uncomfortably as if in sympathy with her.

Next, we asked him a key question: "Would you be willing to make a commitment to learning how to appreciate your wife fully, so that your appreciation makes a real positive difference for both of you?" He said yes, and immediately his wife's eyes opened wide with astonishment. Next, while she watched with growing interest, we gave him several tips and perhaps two minutes of coaching on how to express the same appreciation in a different way.

We showed him a particular way we've found that resonates very well with women—using more detail and direct reports of body sensation. Then we invited him to try again, using the new art form he'd just learned. He did so, speaking a similar appreciation in a very different language. He said, "Thinking of you in that green velvet dress you wore Friday night, I feel a big rush of warmth here in my chest." Although the actual sentence he spoke was hardly ten seconds in length, it had a completely different effect from his first try. This time her breath caught and she burst into tears. She reached over and took his hand, nodding to him through her tears, the color of her face a flushed pink.

The audience was rapt—a pin-drop silence fell over the room, as if the audience knew as one the sacred nature of this moment.

That is the power of appreciating. Although we've seen it hundreds of times all over the world, it always moves us to see its magic work again.

The Fundamental Rationale

Giving a simple, heartfelt appreciation to another person is the quickest way to enhance the flow of positive energy in any relationship. Genuine appreciation, no matter how profound or how simple, always brings about an immediate shift in the quality of a relationship. There is *nothing* more powerful than the clear communication of appreciation. Many times we have been moved to tears by a therapy breakthrough caused by the sudden emergence of a spoken appreciation. One moment the energy in the room will be muddled, frozen, or chaotic. Then someone speaks a simple appreciation. Suddenly the flow of positive feeling connects everyone and takes us all to a new level of harmony.

We have made the same discovery through countless experiments in the sacred laboratory of our own marriage. For people in long-term relationships, appreciating is an especially valuable skill to master. It is an art form of limitless possibility. No matter how richly intimate our relationship has become over the years, we always find new ways of enhancing our skill in appreciating each other. By so doing we add quantum dimensions to the value of our relationship each year it matures.

The same is true for people in new relationships. If single or divorced people can meet and resonate with each other, accompanied by sincere notes of genuine appreciation, they can bring the music of the relationship to life more quickly.

BEGINNING THE ART
OF APPRECIATING

The art of appreciation rests on a few simple principles and practices, which have extraordinary power to move people.

Here's what it looks like in action, drawn from an interaction we had just before this was written. Kathlyn, who loves to cook, had made us a big tossed salad for lunch.

GAY: Thank you for making such a splendid lunch. I appreciate especially your taking the time to make my favorite salad dressing. [For the record, it's a light, creamy dressing made with a lot of chives and garlic.]

KATHLYN: Wasn't that good? The chives came right out of the planter box in the backyard.

GAY: It was fantastic.

Appreciation never gets any more complicated than that, even if you're appreciating a symphony instead of a salad. The essence of the art of appreciation is in its simplicity and sincerity. Although our interchange was completely spontaneous and unrehearsed, it was based on a conscious choice we made more than twenty years ago.

In the early days of our relationship we decided to rewrite many of the scripts we'd witnessed in our childhoods. In reviewing the thousands of interactions we'd witnessed, meals cooked, buttons sewed, school plays attended, we couldn't remember very many instances in which anyone had simply and sincerely appreciated another person. We decided to change all that. We made a decision to base our relationship on the ongoing flow of spoken appreciation. First, we set ourselves the assignment of giving one appreciation an hour to each other whenever we were in each other's presence. It took us months to get to the point at which we were reliably getting our assignment done each day. Eventually, though, appreciating each other out loud became effortless, just part of the flow of everyday life.

Appreciating Is an Action You Take

Appreciating is an active art that can be learned. You can begin to practice the art anywhere, in any relationship, regardless of the degree of intimacy.

Most people live in an impoverished flow of appreciation, both given and received. With practice and a simple map, nearly anyone can move from poverty to abundance in a remarkably short period of time. When appreciating becomes abundant, a new degree of closeness emerges, bringing with it the ability to know the other person's thoughts telepathically and to resonate with his or her emotions.

There are profound gender differences in how women and men *like* to be appreciated, which we'll come back to a little later in the chapter. These radical differences point to clear actions men and women can take to appreciate each other effectively. If you know those differences, you can make significant enhancements in your ability to enjoy a flow of positive energy with others. Here is an example of a gender difference, based on our experiences with teaching the skills of appreciating to many men and women.

In styles of communication, men tend to be digital and women tend to be analogic. To understand this difference, think of a digital watch and an "old-fashioned" analog watch. The digital watch clicks from one second to another in chunks; the analog watch flows from one second to another with the second hand constantly in motion. Men and women operate like that, too. In short, men communicate in chunks, and women communicate in flow.

The Difference Makes a Difference

Practically speaking, this variation in communication styles makes a huge difference in how you appreciate a woman or a man effectively. If you are a man, you will find it works best to speak your appreciation in a flowing manner with detailed references to subtler shades of the emotional palette. A brief digital chunk such as "You look great" or "You smell good" or "Let's have sex" does not often register positively with a woman. It works much better to say something more flowing and subtle, such as "When I see the way your scarf matches your eyes, I get that same warm feeling as twenty years ago when I first saw how beautiful your eyes were."

If you are a woman, you can take advantage of the digital wiring of men by speaking shorter appreciations. "You look great" or "You turn me on" is the type of phrase that registers much more powerfully with men than with women. If you try to give a lengthy, detailed appreciation to a man, you will often be "rewarded" with glazed-over eyes.

Men and women both place different values on the types of appreciation. There's considerable variation among men as well as women, however, so take care not to regard these suggestions as any form of exact science. Couples should experiment with many varieties of appreciation in their relationships. For some men and many women, appreciation by touch is paramount. A caress or a hug means more than any spoken appreciation. For others, the spoken word is the preferred channel. Still others only feel richly appreciated through what we call "gifts of assistance." A gift of assistance is when you discover that your mate has done a load of laundry or taken your car for an oil change.

Everybody needs to learn how to give and receive verbal appreciation. Whether you're a man, a woman, or a child, you can always benefit from the skill of spoken appreciation. The good news is that it's actually a very simple skill. Few of us, however, have had any training in it and are therefore so grossly out of practice that we often fear taking the initial steps.

In an earlier (and considerably hungrier) stage of our careers, we took on the heroic task of a contract with the U.S. Army to teach relationship skills to a large number of their officers. Eventually, even the stiffest of the colonels and generals were delivering and receiving world-class appreciations (although the process of getting them to that point made us feel that every penny of our fee had been earned).

A DAILY SPIRITUAL PRACTICE

The art of appreciation is best thought of as a practical daily spiritual practice. It's a spiritual practice that has immediate, observable results. People grow more beautiful through our appreciation of them. Many people do not realize that the act of appreciating enhances the value of the object of appreciation. They are in the grip of an upside-down error in thinking: They are waiting for the object to become more valuable before they begin to appreciate it. In the real world of human relationships, it works the other way around. You enhance the value of the other person by appreciating him or her. Each of us can choose, at any moment, to initiate the act of appreciating from within ourselves. This act results in an enhanced flow of appreciation in the relationship, which comes back around to make the initiator feel more appreciated.

Here is a beautiful example from one of our clients of the spiritual practice of appreciation in action:

MY HUSBAND gave me the best gift I ever received. Even though we'd been married many years when he gave it to me, and even though it cost no money whatsoever, it resonates through my life every day. The gift was a question.

One day he asked me if he could have a half hour of my time to do something special. Of course I said yes, and he led me to my favorite sitting place by a window overlooking a park outside our apartment. Then, he brought in a pot of a Japanese green tea that I like and set up cups for us on a little table. After all this was arranged, he left and returned bearing an embroidered pillow with a little piece of paper on it, rolled up like a scroll. He ceremoniously placed the cushion before me and indicated I should open the scroll. Inside, in his own hand, he'd written, "How do you most like to be appreciated? What are some specific ways I can show you, every minute or every hour or every day, how much I appreciate you?"

I burst into tears, and he held my hand while I cried. This was so surprising and touching to me, especially considering his background. I don't think his father ever said "thank you" to his mother during the entire time I knew them, so to receive this question from my husband meant to me that he had really broken free of his past. When I recovered, I did my best to tell him some things I thought of. I said, "Tell me simple things as you feel them or notice them. Tell me that you liked something I made you for dinner, and tell me very specifically what you liked about it. Or when you tell me I'm beautiful, which you often do, tell me more specifically what makes you think so. Give me details, details, details—I love details!"

He asked if he could try one right then and get my feedback. He closed his eyes and thought for a moment, then said, "The soup you made last night? I'm still thinking about how deliciously it was spiced. It had some little touch of something in it. I felt so nourished by it afterward."

I felt another tear run down my cheek, recalling that at the last moment I'd added a pinch of marjoram to the soup because I had a feeling it was something he would enjoy and find nurturing. His mother kept an herb garden and often added little touches of fresh herbs to the food she made. I hadn't mentioned the marjoram—and I doubt if he could have named the herb, anyway—but the moment he expressed the appreciation I knew that he had felt it. His body knew.

TELEMPATHY

For us, the discovery of telempathy originally came as a happy surprise. Some years ago we came to a resolution about a money issue that had been troubling us. Each of us had been criticizing the other for spending too much money. The more we found fault with the other, the more faults we found. No matter how much we criticized, our money supply never seemed to increase. After months of struggle, we finally broke through to a new realization. We saw that both of us had inherited impoverished money "scripts" from the past. We decided to stop finding fault with the other person and put our energy into letting go of our old scripts and forming new ideas of how abundant we could be. Everything changed overnight—it was as if a breath of fresh air entered our relationship. But then the real magic happened.

We were enjoying a period of greater closeness since the issue had emerged. Sunday was a day on which Kathlyn often made something special for brunch. One Sunday morning in particular we spontaneously began to express a number of simple appreciations to each other, such as "I really appreciate how you listen to Chris—I've really learned from watching how you do that." The act of appreciating each other brought us even closer.

GAY: Katie asked me if I'd like one of my usual favorites like waffles or pancakes. I tuned in to my body and realized I wanted something lighter, so that's what I told her. She went off into the kitchen and looked through recipe books for a little while. She returned and said, "I'm going to try something new." Suddenly a voice in my mind—not my voice nor Katie's—said "popovers." I blurted out, "Popovers," and Katie's jaw dropped in astonishment. "How did you know that?" she asked.

I said, "I don't know . . . I just knew." The experience was all the more strange because I had no clear idea of what a popover actually was. I had heard the word before and may have tasted them at some point in my life, but just how those popovers "popped over" into my mind I will never know.

We didn't think much more about the experience until a few days later when something similar happened, then another and another. We first thought there was something different about the way we had resolved the money argument. Perhaps we'd done something new that had opened up a level of resonance in us in which psychic events were more likely to occur. Later it occurred to us that it may have been the expressing of appreciations to each other that turned on the flow of connection.

A subsequent experience seemed to confirm the "appreciation theory." It happened on a quiet Sunday afternoon in Colorado.

GAY: I was on the floor, doing some gentle yoga stretches and deep-breathing activities, when I started thinking about my teenage daughter, Amanda, who was away at university. We hadn't been communicating very well, either in person or on the phone, with both of us being quick to snap at each other. I had chalked it up to typical teenage obnoxiousness—in other words, I had been giving her all the responsibility for the problem. Suddenly the idea occurred to me that I might have something to do with the problem. First, I had a good humble chuckle at how long it had taken me— even after many years as a psychotherapist—to hatch this Psych 101 insight. Then, I took ownership of the problem and the anger, giving 100 percent of it to me and 100 percent to her. Because two people were involved, there was 200 percent at stake; however, I'd been giving her the whole 200.

As I did this I was flooded with a series of insights about how I was transferring anger to her that didn't belong to her at all. Some of her actions reminded me so much of her mother that I was unconsciously dumping old anger onto my daughter that was left over from fifteen years before— things I'd apparently never dealt with from my early twenties, during my four-year marriage to my daughter's mother. I felt a smile break out on my face as a feeling of relief spread throughout my body. I had a clear, joyful moment of seeing and appreciating my daughter for being who she was as an individual, free of distortions caused by my old anger-colored perceptions of her.

At that very moment the phone rang. It was Amanda, calling from Maine. Without even saying "hello" she said, "What's up?" She told me she'd been studying when suddenly she got the feeling she "had" to call Dad. I told her about all my feelings and insights of the past few minutes, and she followed by sharing some issues of her own that had been getting in the way. The gates opened and a flow of fresh good feeling surged through our relationship.

These sorts of events started happening with greater frequency. Ultimately we came to a much more comprehensive conclusion: We are all a great deal more telepathic and empathic than we probably imagine. In fact, telepathy and empathy, the deep resonance of the mind and heart, are our natural states of consciousness. We receive this level of resonance free, as our birthright. Later, the stresses of life produce "noise," which obscures our natural telepathy and empathy. We turn off our natural *telempathy*—a mysterious form of communication in which one heart and mind communicate with no spoken words to another heart and mind across time and space—in order to survive in the often confusing and frequently hostile world of growing up. It is often too painful to know the thoughts and feel the feelings of those around us in childhood. So we allow those subtle powers to recede into the background, camouflaged by the noise of social chatter, life's routine busyness, and the compelling images beamed at us by advertising and the media. But we've experienced telempathy ourselves on a number of occasions, as we've shown, and have collected stories from other couples who have also experienced it.

Our experience has shown us that there is no such thing as distance. We are all deeply connected to those we love at all times. The trials of life and the problems of love, however, shift us out of the state of consciousness in which we can feel the essential flow of connection. When we become locked into the problem level, we tend to forget about the connection level where telempathy resides. Einstein pointed out that it is not possible to solve a problem in the same state of consciousness in which the problem was created. We need ways to shift out of the state of consciousness where trials and problems reside, ways of coming back home to the rich flow of organic connection that is our natural birthright.

Appreciating is the best way we've found.

PRACTICING THE ART

In the art of appreciation, simple is good. The best appreciations usually take less than ten seconds. A simple touch on the arm of one you love can communicate more richness than a bushel of pearls and diamonds. We'll give you our favorite tips on how to appreciate, based on what has proved most effective in our seminars and private sessions.

How to Speak Your Appreciations

In our work we focus on spoken appreciations. Although other types of appreciations, such as touch and gifts of assistance, have their place, it's the act of giving each other verbal appreciation that really makes a difference in intimate relationships.

Spoken appreciations need to be fresh, clear, and from the heart. By "fresh" we mean that they need to be based on immediate sensory experience. By "clear" we mean that the appreciation is easy for the receiver to understand. (By the way, the tips we give you here are based on what has worked best with real couples. They are not based on a theory of appreciation we're trying to promote.)

In our seminars we teach an easy way to make sure your appreciations are simple: Keep them to one out-breath. We find that your appreciation is much more likely to be received if you can say it in one breath. One breath is plenty if your appreciation is clear and from the heart. Here's an example:

HIM: I really appreciate how good that spicy perfume you're wearing today smells on you.

HER: I appreciate how you can be strong and gentle at the same time.

Tips and Hints on How to Appreciate Men and Women

Men have a bad reputation for getting tender only when they want to get . . . well, intimate. One tip we'd like to give mainly to men: Careful not to express appreciation only when you want sex. We've probably heard several hundred women say something like, "He only says 'I love you' and hugs me if he wants to go to bed." Be sure to express your appreciation often . . . not just when you're looking for a particular outcome.

Now, a hint for giving appreciations to men: Express shorter appreciations. As we mentioned earlier, men's eyes tend to light up when their partners say things to them like, "You look great" and "Mmmm, you're sexy today." Their eyes tend to glaze over when they hear things like, "I was just thinking of that time on the beach in Malibu when you had that gray cardigan sweater on and you looked so handsome."

Women enjoy being appreciated with rich nuance and plenty of detail. A communication like "You smell good—let's go to bed!" can really move a man. However, it might inspire a woman to move out! Instead, say, "There's a place on your neck that smells heavenly—here, I'll show you exactly where. I wish you could smell it yourself, but I'll try to describe it . . . "

Both men and women enjoy being appreciated through gifts of assistance, but women seem particularly to thrive on them. If you want to appreciate a woman, be sure to look for little things you could do to make her life easier and better. If in doubt about what you might offer as a gift of assistance, just ask. "I'd like to do something that makes your life better and easier. Could you think of something I could do today to express my appreciation for you?" Get in the habit of asking questions like that, and your relationship will blossom.

We've kept a running tally of the kinds of complaints men and women have about each other. Women often complain that men are uncommunicative, out of touch with feelings, messy, and more concerned with sex than emotional intimacy. Men complain that women are critical, stingy with sex, hormonally moody, and too demanding about emotional intimacy. Both genders complain that the other is obsessed with being right and doesn't listen.

Since this debate doesn't seem to be producing any positive results, we suggest that couples simply drop it. Instead, put your attention on appreciating rather than trying to improve the other person through criticism and complaint.

Instead of complaining about a man's tendency to be un-communicative, let's appreciate the good side of that tendency: "I appreciate you for the way you teach me the value of silence." Instead of complaining about a woman's emotionality or hor-monal shifts, appreciate her by saying, "I appreciate you for jolting me out of my rigid, overly logical way of thinking."

Instead of trying to improve a man by criticizing his need to be right, appreciate him for his steadfast loyalty to his point of view. Rather than complaining to a woman for keeping you waiting while she dresses for a party, appreciate her for her attention to details and her concern for aesthetics.

What to Appreciate

Once you open the gateway to appreciating, you'll find many new and wonderful things to notice and celebrate. Here are some of the best ones we've found in the couples whom we've worked with.

• **Essence-Qualities.** Tune in to your partner's singular gifts, unique strengths, and creative aspects. For example, Gay said to Kathlyn not long ago, "I really appreciate how sensitive you are to the needs and feelings of people around you." This is an essence-quality of hers—if it were missing she wouldn't be who she is.

All of us have areas of uniqueness, most of which go uncelebrated throughout our lives. It takes only a few seconds to tune in to the singular, special qualities of your partner and a few seconds more to say an appreciative word about those qualities. Those few seconds, though, can erase a huge number of relationship problems.

• **Helpful actions.** Think for a moment about someone you love. What are some of the things he or she does that makes life better for you or others? Most of us get roundly and frequently criticized for the unhelpful actions we take but are not so well celebrated for the times we perform useful or helpful acts. Let's change all that by putting our attention on the positive.

- **Qualities of body and mind.** What do you appreciate about your partner's looks? What's striking about the way his or her mind works? Does he or she dress a certain way that appeals to you? Does he or she think a certain way that you appreciate? Qualities of body and mind are rich sources of things to appreciate.

- **Daily reliabilities and initiatives.** Most of us have things we do regularly that people rely on. Most of us initiate certain things without having to be reminded of them. For example, around our house Gay handles the daily trek out to the bins while Kathlyn takes care of the flowers. Week in and week out, our house is full of beautiful flowers and never full of rubbish. Until recently, though, we were so in the "rut" of that routine that we didn't think to appreciate the other person for what they did so reliably. Since then we've been more careful to notice and say things like, "Thank you for making the house look and smell so good by taking care of the flowers."

- **Accomplishments and opportunities.** Think for a moment about how you and your loved ones show up in the world. What have been your accomplishments, both large and small? Most people are quite skilled at singling out the failures and missed opportunities of themselves and others. So, we probably don't need much more practice in that area. Most of us, however, do need practice in singling out the accomplishments of ourselves and others, as well as the opportunities we've provided for each other.

- **Relationship and spiritual connections.** Tune in to your partner's relationships with others. Also, tune in to his or her relationship to the cosmos, to the earth, to the spiritual elements of life. Are there things about those relationships that you admire and have learned from? If so, be sure to speak about those things clearly and often.

- **Learning opportunities.** Most of us have learned things of great value from our partners—things we otherwise might never have learned. Sometimes, though, those lessons were accompanied by pain, so that we failed to appreciate the person for bringing us those lessons. Take a moment now and then to think back through the ups and downs of your relationship. What are some of the most powerful lessons you've received from that relationship? Step aside from the pain of those events for a moment and ask yourself: What did I learn that I seemingly was not able to learn until that moment? Express those lessons in the form of appreciations to your partner.

If you're a newcomer to the art of verbal appreciation, it may seem like a daunting project. It all starts with a kind thought and a few simple words, spoken clearly and from the heart. The Action Plan on the following page will help you get started in the real world of your relationships.

Your Action Plan

Your Commitment

"I commit to a quantum positive shift in giving and receiving appreciation."

Your Ongoing Practice

Imagine your partner as an evolving work of art. Picture or feel yourself walking into one of the finest museums in the world and finding your partner featured in the lobby, light streaming through the skylight to reveal some new aspect that you hadn't noticed before. Take a moment to be sensitively aware of your partner's unfolding essence and to appreciate him or her for being in your life.

Your Ten-Second Technique

First, change your body position in some way that allows you to see a new aspect of your partner. For example, soften your eyes, move to the side or back of your partner, or open your posture. Then, express your appreciation in one out-breath by completing the following sentence:

"I appreciate you for _____."

Examples:

- "I appreciate you for remembering to call from work and check in."
- "I appreciate you for the loving way you parent the boys."
- "I appreciate you for listening to my feelings without trying to fix me."

Listener, your job is to complete this sentence:

"I hear that you appreciate me for _____."

Practicing this sentence gives you a chance to really receive the appreciation and to listen free of interpretations or deflections.

If, while giving your appreciations,

you feel any jealousy toward your

partner,

turn immediately to page 231.

A Month's Menu of Appreciations

Living your life from an intention to appreciate is a new and some-what strange idea for many people. Many of us have lived our lives in a context of criticism and judgment so that suddenly switching to a context of appreciation feels like setting off on a journey with no map. For this reason we'd like to offer you a map for the journey—a month's menu of appreciations to get you started on the right path.

The sentences that appear in bold are appreciations that the Giver expresses verbally, with some examples (and writing space) to get you started. You'll also find some types of appreciation activities that are nonverbal. If the Receiver is open to suggestions, ask him/her to take two full, relaxed breaths after receiving an appreciation and say a simple "thank you."

We'll begin by opening the flow of appreciation and generating appreciation for your partner's being or essence, apart from anything she or he does. Giver, some time during the day, make eye contact with your partner and say the following:

Day One

"I appreciate you for being in my life."

Day Two

"One unique quality you have that I appreciate is _____ _____ (your warmth, the quality of your laugh, your commitment to excel-lence . . .)."

Day Three

"I appreciate your skill in _____
_____ (carpentry, writing, singing . . .)."

Day Four

"I appreciate your body and especially your _____
(calves, belly, breasts, butt . . .)."

Day Five

"One aspect of your voice I really appreciate is its _____
(tone, resonance, melody, warmth . . .)."

Day Six

"I appreciate the way you've helped me to grow by _____
_____
(telling the truth even about difficult things, sharing feelings at a deep
level, shifting out of conflicts easily . . .)."

Day Seven

"Something that I really appreciate that you do without drawing any attention to it is _____
_____
(putting the toilet seat down, emptying the trash, putting the clean
clothes away, checking the kids' homework . . .)"

(continued)

A Month's Menu
of Appreciations

Day Eight

Today, verbally appreciate something about your partner's essence to another person.

"One thing I really appreciate about [your partner's name] is

_____

(his or her sensitivity, expressiveness, sense of humor . . .)."

Day Nine

Put a card under your partner's pillow, filling in the following sentence:

"I'm falling in love with your _____

_____ all over again."

Day Ten

"One thing I appreciate that you do, which I've sometimes taken for granted, is _____

_____

(opening doors for me, placing an ample supply of my favorite foods in the refrigerator . . .)."

Day Eleven

"Something about the way you see the world that I appreciate is

_____

_____

(you really like bright color, you enjoy plants, you see the potential in people . . .)."

Day Twelve

"I appreciate the value you place on _____

_____

(staying connected with friends, keeping your space uncluttered, putting creativity first in your day . . .)."

Day Thirteen

Make and hang a banner to greet your partner coming home that completes the following sentence:

"I appreciate the way you create beauty in our lives by _____

_____ (planting bulbs, choosing utensils that feel good in my hands, recycling . . .)."

Day Fourteen

This is an opportunity to appreciate something about your partner that she or he has a hard time appreciating, such as a body part, an old habit, a belief about his or her potential or worth.

"I appreciate your _____

(thighs, productivity, belief that you're not good enough . . .) and am holding a positive intention that you will appreciate it, too."

Day Fifteen

Today take five or ten minutes to sit back to back with your partner and lean against each other as you feel the movement of your breath through your backs. With each out-breath, send appreciation telepathically to your partner for just being.

(continued)

A Month's Menu
of Appreciations

Day Sixteen

"One thing I appreciate about your mind is _____

_____

(how quickly you solve problems, your grasp of the details that usually

escape me, your pipeline to the big picture . . .)."

Day Seventeen

"I appreciate that your creativity has generated _____

_____

(the world's best split pea soup, a new set of bookcases for the kids, op-

portunities for us to work with new companies . . .)."

Day Eighteen

Send a singing telegram (or inscribed balloon message) that com-

pletes the following sentence:

"I appreciate how much you've taught me about _____

_____(loving,

the power of integrity, how to play, the value of telling the truth . . .)."

Day Nineteen

Today you'll focus on the rear view of your partner as she or he

moves around and appreciate something that she or he can't usually see.

"As I watch your back I'm appreciating _____

_____ (the way your hair waves at the

nape of your neck, your butt, the line of the back of your knees . . .)."

Day Twenty

"One thing I really appreciate about your sexuality is _____

_____

(how readily you get an erection, the sensitivity of your touch, the way you dress that shows off your curves . . .)."

Day Twenty-One

Sit with your partner and exchange these phrases two or three times. Appreciate an essence quality of your partner, something that first attracted you.

"I, [your name], appreciate you, [your partner's name], for

_____."

"I hear that you, [your partner's name], appreciate me, [your name], for _____."

Example: "I, Katie, appreciate you, Gay, for your vast vision of possibility."

"I hear that you, Katie, appreciate me, Gay, for my vast vision of possibility."

Day Twenty-Two

"In your interactions with others, I really appreciate the way you

_____

(listen closely, draw out what people really want, are so patient . . .)."

(continued)

A Month's Menu
of Appreciations

Day Twenty-Three

"One of your spiritual qualities that I really appreciate is _____
_____ (your ability
to be still inside, your lovingkindness, your curiosity about life . . .)."

Day Twenty-Four

Let yourself focus today on seeing new things about your partner to appreciate. One way to do this is literally to look at your partner in new ways,
such as relaxing your eyes in your head, looking around your partner's body
rather than directly at him or her, or holding your body in different positions
to watch your partner. Sometime during the day, give your partner a verbal
appreciation that has emerged from your new perspective.

"One new thing I'm noticing to appreciate about you is _____
_____
(the shimmer of your hair, the solidness of your walk, the way light
seems to surround you . . .)."

Day Twenty-Five

"I appreciate all your feelings, your anger, your sadness, your fear, your
sexual feelings, and your joy."

Day Twenty-Six

"One way in which you've grown that I appreciate is by _____
_____
(listening to my feelings, making time to relax and take care of yourself,
learning to speak Spanish . . .)."

Day Twenty-Seven

Spend a few minutes interviewing your partner today about the ways he or she likes to be appreciated most. Consciously give a customized appreciation (e.g., appreciation with a special touch or with eye contact, appreciating your partner in the presence of other people, etc.) before the end of the day.

Day Twenty-Eight

Spend some time today appreciating yourself. Give some sensitive awareness especially to aspects of yourself that in the past you've had trouble appreciating. Some time during the day, tell your partner one thing you appreciated.

**"Today, I generated appreciation for my _____
(baldness, my poor memory, my control tendencies . . .)."**

Day Twenty-Nine

Several times today, think of your partner and send a benign flow of attention in his or her direction.

Day Thirty

"I'm grateful to know you."

Day Thirty-One

"I'm willing to have our relationship grow in value effortlessly."

The Five Secrets at Work

In-Depth Couple's Interview

Here is an interview Kathlyn conducted with a couple with whom she had worked on several occasions. This interview shows what is possible when two people practice the principles in *Lasting Love* over time.

KATHLYN: If you were to sum up everything that's happened into one sentence, what would it be?

MAX: Everything is possible if you make a commitment.

KAY: You have no idea how fast you can make miracles happen, even if you start out with great pain.

KATHLYN: Tell us how it all started.

KAY: I had decided that I was going to break up with Max. The pain was too great. We had been separated for two years, and things had been bad for so long that I did not feel I could stand it anymore.

MAX: One day I had a big realization, that I finally was ready to make a commitment for the first time in my life. I wrote a long letter to Kay about my commitment. I was so excited!

KAY: And I wrote back and said, "Dear Max: No." That was my entire letter.

MAX: When I got the letter I was confused, but then I said to myself, "I am committed to the relationship. How she feels is outside my control. But for me, I am totally committed." I just went on living my life, feeling my commitment. I committed myself to learning everything I could about relationships. That is when I came to your seminar. I then realized exactly what kind of relationship I had always wanted: honesty, integrity, creativity.

KAY: At first I thought all of his commitments were just words—I could not believe him. Then, I saw Max doing all these things to learn about relationships. Finally, one day he said he wanted to ask me the key question, the hard question. He looked me in the eye and asked, "Is there any love left in your heart for me?" At first I could not answer it, then after a few days he asked me again. I said, "No." I actually turned and started to walk away. He then said, "Do you think we have really tried as hard as we possibly can?" He then told me about actions he was taking: quitting his job, moving closer to me, finally making a total commitment to me. That was the starting point for me. At that moment I began to consider again whether I wanted to make such a commitment to him.

MAX: I had taken action to support my commitment. I quit my job and applied for another one near where Kay lived. I did not have the job yet, but I needed to make that action step. This made Kay very curious. She saw me step off into the unknown, no job, no home. Only to be close to her.

KAY: Now it becomes very magical. After I saw these actions I too became committed. Two weeks after that, Max received a message that his elderly uncle wanted to see him.

MAX: He lived in a beautiful villa in the region where Kay lived and worked. I had no idea what he wanted to talk to me about, but when I visited him, he asked me if I wanted his villa so he could enter a nursing home. I was stunned. Two weeks before I had given up my home to move to a new place, and now I was being given the villa of a wealthy man! Now all I needed was a job.

KAY: We decided to renovate the first floor of the villa and turn it into offices where we could work together.

MAX: Now I had my home and my job. All I needed was to convince her to marry me. So I took her to our favorite restaurant. I took her hands and said, "I would like to marry you." She cried but did not say yes or no. I was confused.

KAY: I wanted to say yes, but I also felt much anger come up inside me about money issues and other things we had not worked out. I needed to speak honestly about those things, and when I did, suddenly my whole body said from deep inside, "Yes." I then told Max that I would marry him.

KATHLYN: Kay, it sounds like you needed to be emotionally transparent about your anger before you could discover whether you really wanted to marry Max.

KAY: Yes, one of my biggest fears was being angry. Now, I have learned to just let myself be angry if I'm angry. It's not a fear anymore.

MAX: Something else has happened that seems very big. A while back I made a decision that my first priority would become my relationship with Kay, not my work. Always I had been committed to work first, relationships later. Since I made that decision, everything has changed in a way I would never have suspected. Our income has gone up, even though we are working less. Suddenly there's more time for everything! At the same time I started an appreciation project with Kay. I didn't tell her what I was doing, though. I began saying one or two very clear appreciations every day, like "I appreciate you for making breakfast."

KAY: At first I could not understand what he was doing. Who is this crazy guy?

KATHLYN: And did you begin doing the same after a while?

KAY: It was a long time, maybe six months, but suddenly one day I found myself saying the same kinds of appreciations to Max. This shows Max's genius at work: his persistence. Without it we would not be married, we would not have the baby, we would not have this magnificent life.

Lasting Love Day to Day

Ten Powerful Activities from
Our Seminars

In this section you can learn to put the Lasting Love program to work in your daily interactions. Each of these activities has been tested, reformulated, and retested in the kitchen of our own relationship. We have refined the instructions with the thousands of students, professionals, and couples who have shared their journeys with us, as well. So we know that these activities can create practical magic for you and your partner . . . if you do them.

Some activities include journal writing, some are primarily interactive, while others can be done individually as well as with a partner. We recommend a playful and generous attitude with yourself and your partner as you embark on the journey of whole-body learning. Consider it a new language, let yourself be awkward, and progress in fits and starts. Please put off giving yourself a grade for several months while you experiment and increase your Lasting Love vocabulary.

Here are the activities we'll be exploring.

1. The Yes Breath

2. Renew Your Commitment

3. Utilizing the Power of Commitment

4. Communicating Clearly about Emotions

5. Blame Talk vs. Conscious Heart Talk

6. The Blame Eliminator Process

7. The Art of the Throw

8. Make Friends with Your Upper Limits Patterns

9. Discovering and Expressing Your Creative Genius

10. Appreciation Exploration

Activity 1:

The Yes Breath

One shift in your body-mind can get you unstuck faster than anything else we know. We call this move the Yes Breath because this way of breathing harmonizes your body's physical yes response—nodding—with your emotions and thoughts. You can use the Yes Breath to solve problems, rekindle intimacy with loved ones, and open a whole-body "yes" to more creativity and aliveness.

The Yes Breath also solves the central human dilemma: How can I increase my ability to give and receive more love and appreciation? In our seminars we call this the One Problem; when people start looking at their individual problems as an upper limit to their current capacity for love, they see the power of having a skill that simultaneously takes the brakes off and opens possibilities. The directions follow.

The Basic Yes Breath

Sit comfortably upright. If you are sitting on a chair, come forward so you have space for your back to move without touching the chair. Some people enjoy learning the Yes Breath sitting on large exercise balls. Take a moment to find the bones at the bottom of your pelvis, the sit bones, and to center yourself on them. You might rock back and forth over them to find the centered place. Most people also find it very helpful to have their legs comfortably apart from each other rather than tightly held together. A comfortable distance gives you a solid base on which to easily learn the Yes Breath.

Gently arch and flatten the small of the back, rolling forward and back on your sit bones. Imagine that your pelvis holds a shallow bowl of water, and as you roll forward the water gently sloshes over the front of the bowl. As you roll backward, the water spills over the back rim. The Yes Breath is designed to work best in your comfort zone. If you experience any discomfort, use that as a signal that you are working too hard. Rather than struggling with life and your relationships, the Yes Breath can teach you how to open ease and flow.

When you have found an easy, slow rhythm for arching and flattening your lower back, begin to include the rest of your spine and head. When you roll forward over the sit bones and arch your back, look up slightly, just above the horizon. When you roll backward flattening your back, let your head look down, rounding your whole torso. Stay in your comfort zone and let the movement be very gentle and easy.

Next, add your breathing to the movement. Breathing in and out through your nostrils, notice that the arching of your back invites your in-breath. The rounding of your back gently expels your out-breath like an accordion. Go ahead and cooperate with the Yes Breath, letting the arching draw a deep breath into your belly, and the rounding release your out-breath. Let the top of the in-breath roll right over into the out-breath in a connected way. If you feel like pausing, let your pause come at the bottom of the out-breath. Practice this complete Yes Breath for a minute or two. Now take a moment to rest and notice any shifts in your level of vitality and ease in your body.

Enhancing the Yes Breath

You may practice just the basic Yes Breath and experience more ease and harmony in you and in your partnerships. If you want to enhance the practice, however, the following variations can be added.

While doing the fundamental Yes Breath, alternate between folding your arms over your chest as far as you like, as if embracing and bringing someone close to you, then opening your arms as wide as you like, as if letting the person go. Embrace as you round and breathe out, and release as you arch and breathe in easily and deeply. You can also think of breathing in and opening to your full experience as you open your arms, and breathing out while embracing yourself in this moment. Continue with this practice for a minute or so.

Then, gently reach upward as far as you can comfortably on one side and then the other, as if reaching to pick a delicious fruit just out of range. Harmonize this movement with the Yes Breath by gently arching and reaching, then rounding and releasing. Imagine reaching for your full potential, while enjoying the process of reaching for it. Stay in your comfort zone while giving yourself a full stretch with each reach. Reach so that you can feel it down the side of your body into your hip joint. Take several rounds of reaching and releasing to find an easeful dance between movement and breath. Rest for a moment.

Next, reach and stretch across your body with one arm, then come back to center. Then reach and stretch across with the other arm. Gently arch with your in-breath and reach, round and gather with your out-breath. Reach out in a slightly different direction each time, always crossing the midline of your body then coming back to center before reaching across with the other arm. Rest and notice any shifts in your vitality.

Now, have dessert. Create new connections by playing with moving your joints. Move each of your joints pleasurably in a new way each time. Invent new ways of moving your ankles, knees, hips, shoulders, elbows, wrists, and neck for the next minute or two. Let your movements surprise you. If you find yourself repeating a movement, invent something new. Move two or three joints simultaneously in new ways, as if they were playing a game with each other.

Application of the Yes Breath

1. Think of a recurring relationship problem, something that has repeated three or more times. Remember it vividly and then notice the level of vitality in your body. Then do the Yes Breath until you experience an increase in ease and flow in your body. Continuing with the Yes Breath, bring the issue into your mind again. Breathe and consider the problem at the same time, noticing what happens.

2. If you and your partner get stuck in a discussion, bring creative joint play into your interaction. That is, continue talking while moving your joints in new and pleasurable ways. Most people find this combination gets them unstuck very quickly.

3. Practice several minutes of the Yes Breath before having sex to enhance your connection and pleasure. Continue the Yes Breath if you want to experience the most intimacy.

Activity 2:

Renew Your Commitment

Many couples find that renewing their commitments from time to time gives them a new perspective on the relationship. We have a large collection of thank you notes from people who have used the principles of commitment in our earlier books as the basis of ceremonies they've created. Here are some of the specific commitments they've used for renewal.

Exploration

Read through the following commitments and check the one that you would like to incorporate more deeply into your life and relationships right now.

__ I commit to knowing myself authentically and completely. I commit to regarding every interaction as a learning opportunity. I commit to letting go of any of my defensive postures that inhibit rapid learning.

__ I commit to expressing myself authentically, and to being an opening in which others can express themselves authentically.

__ I commit to the masterful practice of integrity, including acknowledging all key feelings, expressing the unarguable truth, and keeping my agreements.

__ I commit to taking full responsibility for my feelings and the circumstances of my life, and to being a catalyst for others taking full responsibility. Specifically, I take complete responsibility for my physical, emotional, and psychospiritual well-being.

__ I commit to the full embrace and expression of my creativity, and to being a catalyst for the full expression of others' creativity.

__ I commit to living in wonder.

__ I commit to living in essence while acting impeccably in the world.

__ I commit to ease and flow in all aspects of my life.

Say the sentence you chose out loud while moving your wrists and elbows playfully until you feel in harmony with the chosen commitment in your body-mind. Then take a few relaxed, easy breaths.

Action Step

Write this Question for Reflection on each page of your personal daily schedule for the next week.

What am I doing in the gap between the opportunity to commit and the act of committing?

Activity 3:

Utilizing the Power of Commitment

The fastest way to reclaim your power is naming and claiming an *unconscious commitment*. For example, based on the result Tom can see, being fifty pounds overweight, he's committed to being overweight. By naming the commitment consciously, you reclaim the power from the old pattern and break free to make new choices and take new actions. Here's how to do it.

1. Identify an area of relationship conflict or a relationship issue that has recycled in your life.

2. Study the issue to identify the result you are currently creating, and complete the following sentence:

"The result I'm producing is _____."

Examples:

*   . . . working hard and not seeing my family.

*   . . . worrying about money.

*   . . . fighting about chores.

*   . . . getting criticized a lot.

3. The result you're producing will reveal your unconscious commitment. Complete this sentence with your phrase and say it out loud until you experience resonance with the sentence.

"Today is _____ and I'm committed to _____
_____ "

Example:
"Today is Friday and I'm committed to worrying about money."

4. Repeat this phrase with any part of the Yes Breath until you create a shift into more whole-body harmony and vitality. Note that at first you might stop breathing, forget the sentence, or experience all kinds of body sensations. Let yourself gently come back to the breath, and let the breath "iron out" these glitches so you can reclaim the creativity glued to this unconscious commitment.

5. Now create a *conscious commitment* that expresses *what you really want* with this area of your life. First, complete this sentence several times on paper and/or out loud:

"What I *really* want is _____
_____."

Then, complete the following sentence with what you really want and say it out loud until you experience whole-body harmony with your new conscious commitment. You may be surprised to find you have more "hiccups" with this step than with stating your unconscious commitment. You are creating a new future, so give your whole body time to shift in a friendly way.

"I commit to _____

_____."

Examples:

- "I commit to seeing you as my ally."

- "I commit to having plenty of money to do whatever I want and need to do."

- "I commit to creating an easy balance between work and home."

Activity 4:

Communicating Clearly about Emotions

The following communication activity can be done alone or with your partner. Either way, it is valuable practice for the life-long skill of communicating your emotions clearly.

1. Think of a recent relationship issue, or a conflict that has re-curred. For the next two minutes, write in an unedited way about your thoughts, feelings, and perceptions of this issue. (If you get stuck, switch to your nondominant hand, and don't worry if the words are legible or grammatically cor-rect.)

_____

_____

_____

_____

_____

_____

_____

2. Now take a moment to focus your awareness on your specific body sensations. Refer to the body map below and the checklist below and on the next page to help clarify your current experience. Check the sensations that feel closest to your body sensations.

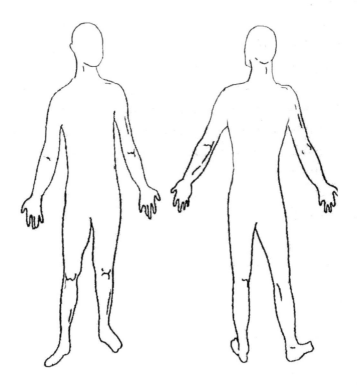

CHECKLIST
BACK OF NECK, ACROSS SHOULDERS, JAW

__ Tight	__ Twisted	__ Pulling
__ Bunched	__ Dense	__ Hot
__ Cordlike	__ Clenched	__ Steely
__ Compressed	__ Blocky	__ Poking

ACROSS HIGH CHEST AND UPPER THROAT

__ Heavy	__ Constricted	__ Pulling down
__ Closed in	__ Congested	__ Lumpy
__ Pressing	__ Achy	__ Searing

AROUND NAVEL AREA

__ Racy, queasy	__ Fluttering	__ Butterfly-ish
__ Nauseous	__ Held in	__ Buzzy
__ Thick	__ Touch-tender	__ Zigzaggy

3. See where you have placed more checks: in the across the shoulders/neck area, upper chest area, or navel area. Condense your issue into a short phrase (e.g., the trash, having kids, enough sex). If you chose the shoulders/neck area, fill in the following sentence with your phrase:

"I feel angry about _____

_____."

If you chose the upper chest area, fill in the following sentence with your phrase:

"I feel sad about _____

_____."

If you chose the navel area, fill in the following sentence with your phrase:

"I feel scared about _____

_____."

4. Say your complete sentence out loud three or four times, emphasizing different words each time. (Note: If you are exploring this activity with a partner, alternate saying your sentences out loud. If you are doing this activity solo, say your sentence out loud to practice whole-body learning.)

5. Say your complete sentence out loud several times, trying different voice pitches and tones.

6. Say your complete sentence out loud several times breathing toward that feeling zone of the body and making gentle movements in the feeling zone: your shoulders, upper chest, or stomach.

7. Take a moment to love yourself for feeling the way you do. Think of someone or something you love without question or condition and give yourself that same love for feeling the emotion you feel.

Say to yourself or out loud: "Today is _____ and I feel _____

_____."

Remember, letting yourself feel creates more flow and ease in you and in your relationships. Allowing yourself to feel any emotion gives you practice in feeling them all.

Activity 5:

Blame Talk vs. Conscious Heart Talk

This activity is designed to be done with a partner. The partner can be a friend, a colleague, or your romantic partner. The first part of this activity has sentences in two columns. The left-hand column contains typical blame statements that we have heard from couples in coaching sessions. The right-hand column gives examples of Conscious Heart Talk, sentences that contain no blame and open intimacy.

BLAME	CONSCIOUS HEART
You're not listening to me.	I wonder how I can communicate effectively.
You're not understanding.	I commit to communicating what I'm saying clearly.
You always criticize me.	I commit to seeing you as my ally.
You don't do what you say you're going to do.	I want to find out how we can keep our agreements with each other.
I'm mad at you for leaving the toilet seat up/down . . . the toothpaste cap off . . . your clothes all over the floor.	I'm mad and what I'm focusing my anger on is these piles of clothes. It may be about some thing else I don't know about yet.

BLAME	CONSCIOUS HEART
Why are they doing this to me?	How am I setting it up so this is happening?
How could he or she have treated me like that?	What do I need to learn from this?
Why were you flirting all night at the party?	I got scared when I saw you talking in the corner.
You never talk to me about your feelings.	I must be withholding some feelings from you. I notice I'm focusing on your withholding.
You're spending too much money.	I'm feeling scared looking at these bills. I'm wondering how to generate enough money to pay for the things we buy.
You never touch me unless you want sex.	I'm feeling hungry for more touch. I want to find a way for us to have more non-sexual touch.

First, each of you separately chooses your favorite blame sentence from the left-hand column. Take turns saying your sentence (it's okay if they are different sentences) out loud four or five times, emphasizing different words verbally and with your body.

Pause and take a few breaths, noticing the racing sensations up the front of your body. We call this glee the "gotcha!" experience that comes from drama and adrenaline. This is the *only* payoff for engaging in the power struggle of "who's right." So appreciate it; this is as good as it gets.

Now, shift to the right-hand sentence directly opposite your chosen blame statement. Please use exactly the words on the page to speak to your partner. Say your sentence while moving your shoulder joints in some new ways you've never tried before. Repeat the sentence again, moving your fingers in some new ways. On the next repetition play with your voice, creating different tones as if you were becoming different instruments in an orchestra. Keep sharing your right-column sentence with each other until you experience a shift into more ease and flow.

You can repeat this cycle with another sentence or two before tackling the next part. The blank lines are for you to write down in the left-hand column the blame sentences you hear or use. The blank lines on the right are for you to create Conscious Heart sentences of your own. Feel free to use the right-hand column of Conscious Heart Talk, on the previous page, to jump-start your creative thinking.

_____   _____

_____   _____

_____   _____

_____   _____

_____   _____

_____   _____

Activity 6:

The Blame Eliminator Process

This process is the simplest, most user-friendly way we know to release the past and step into a future that you consciously choose. The process allows you to organically shift from blame to wonder by liberating the creative energy tied up in old complaints so that you can choose a new future. The power of whole-body learning helps you shift from stuck to energized very quickly.

We have also found that this process can be used successfully with family and friends over the phone. If you share this with another person, be sure to have them engage their whole body in the learning process.

The Blame Eliminator Process

1. Think of a recurring relationship issue that you haven't been able to resolve. Stand in a room where you have some open floor space and complain out loud about this issue or problem for one whole minute. Use lots of gestures and emphasis with your voice and exaggerate your complaint dramatically. (We suggest exaggerating what's wrong first to release the energy bound up in trying to conceal or minimize the complaint. We've found that after people say "No!" emphatically, they feel much more free to find the organic "Yes!")

2. Now, visually pick a place in the room that represents 100 percent responsibility for you. For example, this could be a square on the floor, or a pillow you step onto. When you are ready, physically take a step into 100 percent responsibility. All the Blame Eliminator steps are taken from within this area of 100 percent responsibility.

   (*Note:* If you find yourself wanting to complain again, step out of your 100 percent responsibility area and complain loudly some more. When you are ready, step back into 100 percent responsibility and continue the process.)

3. From within 100 percent responsibility, let your body tell you which direction is the past. Turn and face the past directly. Then complete this sentence out loud four or five times with whatever comes to your mind first:

"From my past, this issue reminds me of _____

_____

_____."

   (*Note:* If you say the sentence and no thought occurs to you, pause, take a breath, and then say the sentence again. After two or three repetitions, what we call "priming the pump," something generally comes to mind so you can finish the sentence.

4. Now, focus your attention on your present life rather than on the past. Complete this sentence four or five times with whatever comes to your mind first:

"I keep this issue going by _____

_____

_____."

5. Next, let your body tell you which direction is the future. *Let yourself start walking or moving into the future.* Keep moving into the future (think of taking your 100 percent responsibility area along with you), as you complete this sentence four or five times out loud with whatever comes to your mind first:

"I can create what I really want by _____

_____

_____."

6. Take a moment to write down your phrases or sentences from step 5, "I can create what I really want by . . . " Take the item that most appeals to you and *explore one measurable action step you can take that will lead you toward what you really want.* For example, you may have generated the phrase, "I can appreciate my partner more." Great idea, but not measurable. The intention behind this very important step is to give your nervous system a concrete goal so that when you have achieved the desired result, you will know it. The important questions are:

• What: _____

_____

_____

• By When: _____

Example:

With "I can appreciate my partner more," here are possible completions:

- **What:** I will deliver five new appreciations to my partner each day for the next week.

- **By When:** Starting tomorrow morning.

Activity 7:

The Art of the Throw

Our students and colleagues have told us that learning to use the Art of the Throw in their relationships has produced more creativity than any other tool.

One friend told us that when she first began practicing this simple art, she was very skeptical about its usefulness. She persisted for a few days and was astonished to find how much fun she and her partner were having in solving problems and working on projects together. She recently told us that she keeps discovering more areas in which to apply what she now considers one of her top tools. Allow yourself to have as much fun as you can with this tool.

The Basic Throw

Creativity stops in most relationships because somebody drops the ball in conversation. Wonder and synergy also stall when the ball isn't thrown in the first place, but is hooked, slammed, or dunked with an "I win!" attitude. The Art of the Throw crafts an intimate game and keeps it going, two benefits that accelerate cocreativity.

Designate a practice time of five minutes or so when you want to develop more skill in throwing. The speaker chooses any topic of conversation. The listener practices throwing. Speaker, do your best to speak in one-out-breath sentences, then wait for the throw. Listener, select from the following verbal "throws" after each communication from the Speaker. Give each of you equal time to be the Speaker—about two minutes.

- Tell me more about that.

- What interested you most about that?

- Hmmm . . . I wonder how you experienced that.

- Then what happened?

- I'm curious to hear more.

- I heard you say [summarize the gist of what you heard with an attitude of curiosity].

- It sounds like you felt [excited, sad, scared, anxious, mad, etc.].

Here's an example:

SPEAKER: I had a rough time at work today.

LISTENER: Tell me more about that.

SPEAKER: Well, the meeting didn't go at all like I planned, and Jim interrupted me right out of the gate and acted like the idea was his.

LISTENER: It sounds like you felt mad.

SPEAKER: You bet, and I was also kind of stunned—I thought we were teaming up on this one.

LISTENER: Then what happened?

Notice what is *not* happening in this exchange. The Listener is not trying to interpret, fix, or analyze what the Speaker is saying. The Listener is practicing the Art of the Throw, an art that cultivates curiosity and deeper intimacy.

The Problem-Solving Throw

Stand facing your partner. Designate the first Leader. You both will throw in this activity.

• Leader, think of an unresolved issue, something you'd like to clear up. Let your face take on an exaggerated expression of the way you experience this issue right now, such as a scowl or pursed lips or *Home Alone* face.

• Now throw this facial expression to your partner. Think of the expression like a mask that you can actually throw.

• Partner, catch and try this exaggerated expression on your face for a moment. Then make some change in the facial expression and throw it back to the Leader.

• Leader, receive and try on the expression, then make some change in it and throw it back.

• Throw and change several times until the Leader experiences a shift in the issue. (The shift could be a lightening up or loosening of the grip of the problem, a solution, or a sense of curiosity rather than a feeling of being stuck.)

Here are some variations:

• You can extend the throw to include whole-body gestures and postures that you throw back and forth. Explorers have reported generating more fun and creativity when they use a whole-body throw. Then switch leaders and repeat the activity.

• Each of you can throw body sensations or tension from one part of your body to another until the stress loosens up. Remember, the quickest way to change your mind is to change your body.

The Creative Throw

Sometime when you are working on a project or want to generate some new ideas, use this movement activity.

One of you think of the project and use your hands to sculpt the air in front of you into a shape that matches your experience of it right now. Then throw the shape to your partner. Partner, reshape the sculpture, and throw it back. Make a few throws, then add a word to the throw each time. Continue to throw and sculpt a few times until you reach a satisfying completion.

Activity 8:

Make Friends with Your Upper Limits Patterns

Ask yourself, "What has happened when things are going well in my close relationships?" Is there anything that you do or experience that diminishes your good feeling or the harmony in your relationships? Wonder about the ways in which you ride the positive energy roller coaster over the top into a slide, funk, or conflict. These are your Upper Limits patterns.

Here's a sample list:

- Worry thoughts, especially anticipating how things are going to go wrong in the future

- Broken agreements, such as agreeing to give appreciations three times this week and "forgetting"

- Hurrying

- Criticism of my partner or myself

- Bumping into things and dropping stuff

- Interrupting

Now make a list of your top five favorite Upper Limits behaviors:

1. _____

• _____

2. _____

• _____

3. _____

• _____

4. _____

• _____

5. _____

• _____

Now take a few moments to breathe easily and gently into your relaxed belly with the Yes Breath, then say these sentences out loud four or five times each:

"I am willing to make friends with my Upper Limits problem."

"I commit to learning from my Upper Limits behaviors in a friendly way."

Action Step

Next to each item from your Upper Limits list, create an action or practice that you can shift to when you notice the Upper Limits problem rearing its head. Here are some examples:

* Worry thoughts, especially anticipating

  ACTION: Notice the body sensations that arise when I worry, and take two to three Yes Breaths into that part of my body.

* Breaking agreements with my partner

  ACTION: Tell the truth about the broken agreement, feel my feelings, and listen to my partner's feelings; make a new agreement.

* Hurrying

  ACTION: Breathe toward the body sensations of hurry-up where I experience it most strongly in my body.

* Criticizing my partner

  ACTION: Deliver five appreciation expressions on the spot.

* Bumping into things and dropping stuff

  ACTION: Get a massage, go dancing, take a beach walk, or take a long bath.

• Interrupting

ACTION: Acknowledge the interruption, and make a new commitment to listen with the Art of the Toss.

Now consider this Question for Reflection: How can I give and receive more love and positive energy every day?

_____

_____

_____

_____

_____

Activity 9:

*Discovering and Expressing
Your Creative Genius*

According to the dictionary, genius means having "a great natural ability; a great original creative ability; a strong disposition or inclination." Let's explore this further.

Step One

Begin this exploration with a few moments of stretching and breathing until you feel greater ease and flow in your body. Then fill in or complete the sentences below, pausing to reconnect with the relaxed breathing between each sentence.

• When I'm _____

_____,

it doesn't seem like work at all (e.g., teaching something I've learned to others).

• Ever since I was a child, I've loved to _____

_____

(e.g., make up stories).

• In my work I get the best results when I'm _____

_____

(e.g., moving around and not sitting in one place).

• My close friends and associates tell me that one of the most

unique capabilities I have is _____

_____

(e.g., the ability to think on my feet).

• When I'm working, time seems to just disappear when I'm

_____

_____

(e.g., collaborating with one or two other people).

Step Two

Take your phrases from step one and list them separately:

_____

_____

_____

_____

_____

Now construct a unique introduction of yourself combining the most interesting phrases from what you just wrote.

Play with combinations of phrases and words until you condense them into a one out-breath phrase:

_____

_____

For example: "Hi, I'm Katie, and I love to feel through to the heart and inspire creative play." (I introduced myself to a producer at a Hollywood party this way and had the most animated conversation I can remember at a social event.)

Action Step

Each day for one week, use this phrase out loud to at least one different person in a public setting (talking to your pet counts for only one day). Then consider this Question for Reflection: Am I willing to commit to the full expression of my creativity?

Activity 10:

Appreciation Exploration

Use this inner journey to expand your ability to appreciate yourself and your partner. We suggest doing this activity while you are comfortably seated with eyes closed. You can record the instructions to play aloud or read them to each other.

Consider yourself an evolving work of art (pause for a Yes Breath or two). . . . Imagine walking into a brand new museum and finding yourself featured in the foyer under a large skylight. . . . Give yourself the same kind of sensitive attention you would give to a priceless work of art. . . .

What kind of masterpiece are you? Are you more like a kinetic sculpture or a large oil painting? Are you a song or a performance art piece with constantly changing features? Are you more like an illuminated manuscript with golden edges? Are you a series of photographs across the entire entrance? Let yourself acknowledge and appreciate your unique brilliance in the world, a form like no other. Take a few slow, relaxed breaths to embrace your uniqueness.

See if you would be willing to release any further attempts to take yourself on as an improvement project. Just as you wouldn't think of going into the Louvre Museum in Paris and improving one of the Rubens paintings, let go of any further struggles with improving yourself . . . and take yourself on for the rest of your life as an appreciation project. Take some gentle belly breaths as you get deeply willing to turn your whole attention to appreciating yourself. Be sensitively aware of your body sensations right now. Bring sensitive attention to any feelings arising. Give some appreciation to the thoughts moving through your mind.

Now release your partner as your personal improvement project. Take a final scan through all your attempts to change and fix your partner. Hold all those attempts in one of your hands as if holding an old lunch pail. Take a breath and open your hand, releasing the past. Take a few relaxed, easy breaths as you now take on your partner as an appreciation project. Let your whole body expand to the new task of appreciating your partner. Think of one aspect of your partner that expresses his or her essence, who he or she is at the core. Give your sensitive awareness to this quality, embracing it and breathing to acknowledge your partner's essence. See if you would be willing to make appreciating your fall-back position with yourself and your partner. When all else falls away, appreciating remains. Breathe and expand in appreciation.

Relationship ER

*Rapid Solutions for Urgent
Relationship Concerns*

We'd like to thank you for joining us in this exploration of the real world of conscious relationships. We've had the pleasure of training more than a thousand coaches and therapists during our careers, as well as working directly with about thirty-five hundred couples so far. The material in this appendix is drawn from the front lines of real life. One of our colleagues joked that it contains the relationship equivalent of "what to do when the building's on fire," but in a way he's absolutely right.

One of the best compliments we ever received came from a woman who said to us after a session, "Thank you for giving me such a clear, straight answer. It's what I really needed. I appreciate that you actually answered my question rather than doing the usual 'therapy thing.'" The question she had asked was, "How can I tell when my husband is lying?" Instead of doing the usual "therapy thing" of asking her how she felt about her husband's habitual lying, we decided to give her a ten-minute crash course in how to tell when people are lying. The information turned out to be of great use to other clients and to our trainees. We began to collect other urgent information, which you now have before your eyes. The material addresses major issues people bring to relationship coaching sessions. Here are eight issues we'll be exploring.

1. How to spot when your partner is lying by learning to spot the Three Red Flags that signal concealment

2. How to know when it's time to leave a troubled relationship

3. The single most important move to attract a healthy, conscious relationship into your life

4. How to tell difficult truths so that people thank you afterwards

5. Constellation, the game of relationship harmony

6. Clarity, the one-minute communication tool

7. How to eliminate jealousy from your close relationships

8. How to grow a conscious relationship

Issue 1:

How to Spot When Your Partner Is Lying

We have developed strong opinions about the value of honesty in relationships. In a word, honesty is *crucial*. Crucial is derived from the same word that means *crux*. And honesty really is the crux of the matter in close relationships. The bottom line: Lying creates distance and conflict; honesty creates closeness and harmony. As we discussed in chapter 3, if there is any significant truth you haven't communicated to your primary partner, you forfeit the right to expect a good relationship with him or her until that truth is told. Most people don't realize this, so when things aren't going well in the relationship, they think the other person is the source of what's wrong, instead of looking for withheld truths on their own part.

At our lectures and seminars, people often ask: "How can I tell if my partner is lying?" Usually our response is, "Don't worry about your partner—put your attention on whether *you're* concealing any lies!"

There *is,* however, a reliable way to find out if your partner is lying, and we will describe it for you as best we can. Understand, though, that the following techniques, while quite reliable, can never be regarded as an exact science. Like everything involving complex human behavior, there is considerable individual variation.

Step One

First, make sure you really want to know the truth. These techniques work very quickly, so before using them you need to be sure you choose honesty over illusion. Some people prefer the state of "blissful ignorance," while others prefer to know the truth even if it makes them uncomfortable. We definitely recommend the latter as a path to healthy, conscious living.

Step Two

Think carefully about the exact question you want answered. Sex and money are the two subjects partners lie about most. In order to get at the truth, your question, regardless of the subject, needs to be specific. For example, don't ask, "Do you find Pat attractive?" if what you really want to know is, "Have you had sex with Pat?"

Step Three

Learn the Three Red Flags that signal concealment. Here's what to look for.

Red Flag #1: Body Language Indicating Concealment. In the first few seconds after you ask your question, notice if your partner shows any of the following body language:

• Face-Touching

When you ask the question, does he or she suddenly touch the face or cover part of it? (Think back to Bill Clinton saying he didn't have sex with Monica Lewinsky—he reached up and touched his nose immediately after saying it.)

• Arm/Leg Shift

Does the person suddenly change the position of his or her arms or legs? Two common reactions: crossing arms over chest quickly and crossing one leg over another.

• Eye Shift

When you ask the question, does he or she shift eyes away from contact or lock into a hard stare of excessively intense eye contact?

• Body Turn

Does the person turn his or her body away from you slightly?

Red Flag #2: Voice Mannerisms Indicating Concealment. When you ask a question that exposes a lie, your partner's voice will often give clues to the real truth. Listen for these reactions in the first few seconds after you ask the question:

• Pitch Shift

Does the person's voice suddenly go up or down in pitch?

• Speed-Shift

Does he or she suddenly begin speaking faster?

• Ums and Ahs

Does the person cough, clear the throat, or fumble around vocally with a sudden increase in filler words such as "er," "um," and "uh"?

Red Flag #3: Attitude Reactions Indicating Concealment. Instead of answering a question with the simple truth, your partner may defensively avoid the question with a sudden display of attitude. Watch for these reactions in the first few seconds after asking a question:

• Hostility

Does he or she react with hostility? (For example, you ask, "Have you had sex with Pat?" and your partner responds with, "Why the hell would you ask a thing like that?" instead of a simple yes or no.)

• Indignation

Does he or she react with indignation? (You ask, "Have you had sex with Pat?" Your partner responds with, "I'm offended that you could even think such a thought!")

• Turnaround

Does he or she respond to your question with a question instead of an answer? (You ask, "Have you got any bank accounts I don't know about?" Your mate responds with, "Why are you asking something like that right now?")

Step Four

Before asking the big question, first get a baseline by noticing if your partner shows any Red Flags when you ask innocuous questions. Ask a simple yes-or-no question your partner is not likely to lie about: "Do you want eggs this morning?" or "Do you know when the soccer game is this week?" Watch the reaction carefully. You probably won't see any Red Flags in response to an innocuous question, but you need to get a baseline to find out if your mate does any of the Red Flags under normal, non-lying circumstances.

Step Five

Pop the crucial question and watch the reactions. Be mindful of timing, though. Don't do any of this while either of you are driving or operating equipment of any kind. If you have children, make sure you ask the question when they're not likely to be influenced by any heated words that might ensue.

Going Forward

In our experience, the lie itself is just the tip of the iceberg. The real issues that need to be confronted are those that gave rise to the lie. Lies can be a force for destruction or a springboard to positive breakthroughs, depending on how you handle the aftermath. Chapter 5, on creativity, is worth careful study if you uncover a pattern of lies in a relationship. In working with many couples in the aftermath of a suddenly discovered lie, we have found that there was almost always a point much earlier in the relationship when one or both people chose to ignore a creative urge. For example, we worked with a couple who caught each other having affairs. Actually, she caught him first, then revealed hers to him in a counseling session afterwards. Over several sessions, however, it became clear that both of them were using the affairs to enliven the stagnation they both felt from a creative urge they'd ignored a year earlier. They had both wanted to move to a different part of the country but had decided not to do so for financial reasons. Understanding the affairs in this context, they revisited the issue of whether to move (and eventually did).

The aftermath of a discovered lie is a good time to seek the counsel of a third party such as a relationship coach. There is a strong tendency to engage in blame and recrimination at such a time; friends and family members, while giving support, often fan the flames of blame. A clear-headed counselor can often bring the essential learning opportunities to light much faster than friends and family members.

Issue 2:

Should I Go or Should I Stay?

In thirty-plus trips around the world teaching relationship seminars, we've been asked the following question perhaps more than any other: "How can I know when it's time to leave a troubled relationship?" It doesn't matter whether we're in Calcutta or Chicago or Copenhagen—someone almost always raises a hand to ask this question.

We know how difficult this question is to answer because we've both asked it ourselves in our painful relationships of the past. Oftentimes the person who asks it has so much pain written on his or her face that we first ask the person to pause for a moment to acknowledge that pain. We invite the person to take ten seconds to experience the feelings of self-acceptance and self-appreciation for weathering the great difficulties that have obviously given rise to the question in the first place.

This suggestion is actually a first step in answering the question for yourself. Before making any difficult choice, it's important to love and honor yourself for everything you're feeling on the emotional level. This means taking a moment to honor your fear, your anger, your grief, and the pain of the unmet potential of the relationship. We begin new relationships with high hopes, and the failure to realize the potential we see at the beginning can be one of the most painful parts of breaking up.

The Big Question

We've found that one question can provide a great leap forward in helping you make the decision of whether to leave or stay. To answer it, you need to go deeply inside yourself to consult your own inner emotional world. You need to feel the pain that's living in your body, and you need to compare that pain to the feeling of positive potential. Then ask yourself this question:

Does the pain you feel about the relationship overshadow the potential you feel?

The reason this question is so helpful is that many people stay too long in a troubled relationship because they're clinging to a slender thread of hope *while denying and ignoring the growing mountain of pain that's accumulating in their bodies.* That's why so many people get physically sick (not to speak of emotionally drained) as they endure more and more pain from a difficult relationship. Hope is a powerful motivator, but it can also be a powerfully addictive drug. Living in hope, while ignoring or denying the growing reservoir of pain in your body, can be hazardous to your mental and physical health. Often, when we ask people this question, we can see the answer immediately on their faces. Often people will begin to cry as they acknowledge the deep pain they've been living with. There is, however, always a look of relief that appears on their faces as they acknowledge part of themselves they've been hiding or denying.

A Secondary Question

There is a second question that can be useful in making the fateful decision of whether to leave or stay. Before asking the question, we ask people to transport themselves to an imaginary future a year from now. We ask them to look back from this imaginary future to where they are now and ask: Do I wish I'd left or stayed?

About four times out of every five, people who ask this question realize they've wanted to leave for a very long time. When we ask them to go into the imaginary future they suddenly realize that it's a disservice to themselves to stay any longer. They wish they'd left. Others realize that it's not time to go just yet.

Of course, there are many practical considerations that go into a decision to leave relationships: children, possessions, money, family connections. Most people, however, obsess on those issues without first consulting the depths of themselves and asking, Do *I* want to go or stay? Once you're clear about what you want, it's much easier to handle the practical considerations. Here again, a third party can often make a world of difference in helping you move through this time of crucial decisions.

Issue 3:

The Single Most Important Move

There is a piece of priceless wisdom that we've seen change the lives of many single and divorced people. We first learned it ourselves the hard way, by struggling through many difficult relationships in our twenties and early thirties. Once we realized it and put it into practice, we met each other and found the relationship of our dreams. We offer it to you, in hopes that it will work its magic on you.

Here it is:

The major barrier that stands in the way of our establishing a loving relationship with another person is an unloved part of ourselves. A hidden aspect of ourselves that we have never fully loved and accepted keeps us from bringing genuine love into our lives. Even if we bring a healthy new relationship into our lives, this unloved part of ourselves can rush forward to prevent us from enjoying and keeping the new love we feel.

Here's why:

If you don't love yourself, you'll always be looking for someone else to do it for you. It never works, though, because people who don't love themselves attract other people who don't love themselves. Then they try to get others to love them unconditionally when they're not even doing it for themselves.

When you love yourself deeply and unconditionally for everything you are and aren't, you attract people who love and accept themselves deeply and unconditionally. If you feel fundamentally unlovable deep down inside, you'll attract a lover who feels the same way.

When we don't love some part of ourselves, we run around in desperation trying to get someone else to love us. Our hope is that if they give us enough love our unlovable part will go away. It never does. Only a moment of loving ourselves unconditionally will do that particular job.

Most of us spend our lives running from that unlovable part of us. When we finally confront it, we will usually discover it's a fear. It's usually a particular fear, and there are only a very small number of them.

One of them is fear of abandonment. You can probably see why that fear could play havoc in your relationships. As we showed you in chapter 3, it certainly did in our early relationships, before we became aware that this fear was driving a lot of our troublesome behavior. When you're afraid of being left alone, you'll either keep people distant so it won't hurt so badly if they leave you, or you'll cling to them so completely they can't leave without dragging you with them.

Another big fear is the dread of being smothered by the other person. When you're in the grip of this fear, you're worried that your individuality and freedom will be lost if you surrender to a full union with the other person. So, you stay at arm's length, just as a person who's afraid of drowning might stand a yard or so away from the water's edge.

The good thing to know about fear is that it's simply a pulsating quiver of racy-queasy sensations in your stomach area. Fear, said the legendary psychiatrist Frederick "Fritz" Perls, is merely excitement without the breath. Breathe into the fear and watch what happens: The butterflies will flutter out of hiding and fly away.

When you love that fear directly, you can actually feel it disappear. In the space where the fear used to be, you now feel a big open space into which a wonderful new relationship can enter. That's what happened to us, and that's what we've seen happen to a lot of people when they mustered the courage to love themselves and all their fears.

The Grip of Fear Holds Us in Check

It's impossible to enjoy good relationships until we give that scary place in ourselves a split second of love. The reason: The fear causes us to push people away when they get too close. That's because our fear gets stirred up when we let people in. To keep the fear under control, we keep people at a distance. We push down the very aspects of ourselves that most need to come to the surface and be loved. Then, having already judged ourselves unlovable, we strain to get others to love us. Trying to get other people to love us when we don't think ourselves lovable is like a dog chasing its own tail. The more they try to love us, the faster we run from it.

Fortunately you can solve that problem right now, right here.

What are you feeling right now? Tune in to yourself and do a quick body scan. Are you afraid that the ideas in this book may not work for you? Are you afraid that nothing will work? Are you worried that maybe you're not good enough to do this? Do you fear, as we once did, that there's something fundamentally wrong with you that is always going to keep you from love?

Right now feel all these feelings and *love* them. Love yourself for having them. Love yourself for your courage to feel.

We've never met anyone who loved themselves deeply and unconditionally all the time. Don't expect that you'll be perfect at it, either. Begin with a second or two of loving yourself and work up from there. Begin with a commitment to loving yourself. That way, you'll have the commitment to fall back on when you find yourself in the grip of your unlovable part.

Remember, too, that loving yourself has nothing to do with egotism or self-flattery. Egotistical people are desperately trying to get other people to love them, even though they feel deeply unlovable inside. That's why egotism and boasting look so tacky: Everybody knows they're phony.

We're talking about genuine, sincere, heartfelt, and humble love for yourself. It's a feeling of accepting yourself for everything you are and everything you aren't. Unless you're superhuman, you won't ever feel absolute love and acceptance for yourself all the time. You can, however, make a commitment to feeling that way. Making a commitment to loving yourself gives you firm ground to stand on throughout the ups and downs of your life.

Right now say to yourself:

"I commit to loving myself deeply."

Float the idea around in your mind and feel it in your body. Use it as an anchor in your work on yourself.

Issue 4:

How to Tell Difficult Truths

There is a piece of wisdom about life and relationships so important that it should have been posted on the walls of our elementary schools and taught us every day: Our lives are shaped by the significant truths we say or don't say. Most of those life-defining truths can be spoken in ten seconds with one out-breath. Think of the difference in the life of Bill Clinton and all of us in America had he said, "Yes, indeed—I had lots of sex with that woman." That's an example of a ten-second, one-out-breath truth that would have saved this country considerable time and money. Instead, in the aftermath of a ten-second lie, "I didn't have sex with that woman," came $50 million worth of hassle and a year of partisan bickering, not to mention the unknown personal cost to Bill Clinton and his family.

Most of our truths are not the $50 million kind, but in the context of our lives they have that same level of importance. That's why it's important to learn how to speak the truth. The barrier most people face in speaking the truth is that they don't want to do it in a way that hurts other people and stirs up trouble. From three decades of helping people speak difficult truths to each other, we've learned that the following few simple techniques and principles can make the process much easier.

When You Speak the Unarguable,
People Don't Argue

If I were to say to you, "My stomach feels queasy," you'd have a difficult time arguing with me. But, were I to say to you, "You make me sick to my stomach," you'd probably find plenty to argue with in that sentence. The difference is intention.

If I say, "My stomach feels queasy," my intention is to reveal my inner experience. If I say, "You make me sick to my stomach," my intention is to blame you for my experience. In speaking difficult truths so that people thank you afterwards, the trick is to reveal your inner experience and stay out of blame. Breakthroughs in relationship communication are always brought about by saying unarguable things and never by blaming, as we discussed in chapter 4. It's possible to communicate the most difficult truths in this new way, so that people are literally filled with gratitude afterwards.

The Technique

The trick is to speak first from your three major feeling zones. Zone 1 is made up of your neck, shoulders, and midback. When you're tense in this zone it's because you're holding onto anger you haven't communicated. Zone 2 is your throat and chest. This zone tells you when you're feeling sad by signaling you with constriction ("lump in the throat") and a sense of heaviness. Zone 3 is your stomach and beltline. Tension and racy-queasy sensations ("butterflies") tell you that you're scared.

Let's say you want to break up with your lover. Your main complaints are that he never helps around the house, he has a perfect record of forgetting your birthday, and he is unwilling to make a long-term commitment to the relationship.

Scenario One

You say to him, "I'm leaving you because you're lazy, disrespectful, and commitment-phobic."

Would he be likely to thank you for sharing this "truth" with him? Probably not. He'd probably argue with all three of your labels for him. You've provided him with a perfect way to avoid learning anything from your communication because you've communicated it in arguable terms.

Scenario Two

You say to him, "For a long time I've been feeling sad and disappointed. I can feel it right now in my chest, and I can hear it in my voice. I don't think I'm getting what I want in our relationship. I feel angry a lot at you, and although I feel scared about being by myself, I think I'd rather face that fear than continue to feel what I've been experiencing the past year."

There's no guarantee he'll thank you for speaking those truths, but we can give you a pretty solid guarantee that he won't argue with you. We know, because we've coached hundreds of people to speak like that in sessions, and it stops arguments cold.

With regard to thanks, we've seen many situations in which people felt upset at hearing unarguable truths. They registered the impact of the communication, however, and learned from it. Later, when they've digested it thoroughly, they often thank and appreciate the speaker for being courageous enough to speak the truth in a way that didn't produce arguments.

Issue 5:

Constellation

Constellation is one of the most powerful ways we've discovered to open up a deeper flow of positive energy and love in your life. It's the deepest kind of learning, yet it's also completely friendly.

Constellation is like nothing else you've ever done. The best way to discover its remarkable power is to go right ahead and experience it yourself. Understanding it conceptually first doesn't make a whit of difference, and after you experience Constellation you won't need any explanations. It's as if you suddenly looked up one night and saw the Milky Way constellation for the first time. Even though someone might have tried to explain it to you earlier, that first moment of seeing it for yourself was what counted.

As you move consciously through the steps, Constellation slowly begins to make sense to your whole being, not merely to your intellect. Then it begins to make a whole lot of sense. Then . . . WHOOSH! Suddenly a vast open space of ease opens up. You feel a glow of spacious well-being inside you, and you feel a new flow of love and lightness in your relationships.

You can play Constellation by yourself or with your partner. Playing with a partner is highly recommended. If you play "solitaire" you'll need to use your imagination a little bit more than if you're playing with a partner.

If you'd like to experience Constellation, get your ticket and proceed. The ticket's free, but you have to put everything on the line in order to get one.

Step One

Heartfelt commitment is your entry ticket. Constellation begins the moment you commit.

The great thing about commitment is that you can't fake it. You can hear yourself make a commitment in your mind, and you can feel in your body when you make a commitment . . . but it's the results that let you know if your commitment means anything.

If you commit to fasting on vegetable juice all day, you might feel that commitment in your body. You might think you made a sincere commitment. However, if you have three Big Macs, a Whopper, and a large Coke for breakfast an hour later, your actions will tell you whether your word and your inner feelings have any value in predicting your behavior.
Right now, consider the following commitment:

I commit to experiencing love, clarity, and enlightenment through every relationship interaction I have, now and forever.

I specifically make a commitment to feeling love, clarity, and enlightenment in situations where I might typically get defensive.★
I commit to completing the steps of Constellation.

(★Common defensive maneuvers: denying, playing dumb, hiding truths, scaring people with your anger, over-intellectualizing, justifying your actions, being superreasonable, changing the subject, getting hysterical, getting rigid, getting sick)

If this commitment doesn't sound like something you want to make, we'll part company now. Blessings to you on your journey.

If you embrace this commitment, however, write it out in the following format:

I, [your name], commit to experiencing love, clarity, and enlightenment in each relationship interaction I have, now and forever.

I, [your name], specifically commit to feeling love, clarity, and enlightenment in situations where I might typically get defensive.

I, [your name], commit to completing the steps of Constellation.

_____

_____

_____

_____

_____

Signed _____

Dated _____

Witnessed by _____

As soon as you've done that, you're welcome to play Constellation. Congratulations! You're on your way to the stars.

Step Two

Make a bubble diagram. In seminars, we use a big piece of paper about a metre square, and we suggest making the bubbles about the size of a table tennis ball. However, you're welcome to use any size of paper or bubble you like. You may try it out on the next page for starters.

Put your bubble in the middle and write me in the middle of the bubble.

For your next bubble, think carefully about the living person you consider to be your closest relationship. Write the person's name in the bubble, and locate the bubble nearest to your bubble.

Now, think of the next-closest living person in your life. Write his or her name in a bubble, and locate that bubble in a spot that indicates the appropriate degree of closeness.

Do the same with a third living person.

Now we will shift to people both living and dead. Locate your mother in a bubble, and place the bubble in a location appropriate to how close your relationship with her is or was. Do the same for your father. (If you didn't know one or both your parents, locate the person's bubble in a place that symbolizes for you the degree of closeness or distance you feel or felt.)

Do the same for brothers, sisters, and other significant friends and family members who were around when you were growing up.

For each person you've "bubbled" so far, give the person an energy rating. The Energy Scale goes from –3 up to +3. Here's how to estimate each person's Energy Rating:

My Bubble Diagram

-3. A lot of conflict in the relationship. Maybe you don't or didn't speak. Perhaps you were in a lawsuit against the person. Maybe you avoid the person entirely.

-2. You argue. Conflict characterizes your relationship. You think of the relationship as a significant source of conflict.

-1. A slight or modest amount of conflict. You feel tension around the person, but not much outright hostility.

0. Neutral. Not really positive or negative.

+1. Benign feelings. Pleasant to be around the person. Mostly positive relationship, with only minor conflicts.

+2. Like or love the person a great deal. A close friend, a beloved relative.

+3. Deep love. Important beyond words. A beloved mate or essential person.

A person will often have both a positive and a negative number. For example, your deepest love relationship may be a +3 and a -3 at the same time. Others may have only a positive or a negative number.

Write your Energy Rating next to each person's bubble.

When you finish, take a moment of rest and reflection. Ask yourself: What have I learned so far? If you're doing Constellation with one or more other players, share what you've learned with each other.

Step Three: Worst You, Best You

Pick a bubble to work with first. Don't pick your closest love-partner yet. Start with another relationship. For the purposes of the game, it needs to be a person with whom you have some conflict . . . perhaps a –2 or a –3 on your Energy Rating scale. The person can have a +2 or +3, too, but you need a relationship with some conflict to do the next part of the game.

In your imagination, put yourself in that person's place. What is the worst thought or utterance you think this person might have ever thought or said *about you*? Use your imagination, or recall the memory of a specific incident.

For example, the worst thing Gay can imagine his mother saying or thinking about him is, "Your very existence ruined my life." She might not have ever said it out loud, but it seemed to be in the background of a lot of hot conversations when Gay was growing up.

Now put it in the form of a short statement that starts with You:

"You're hopeless, you're stupid, you'll never amount to anything, you're worthless, you're no daughter/son of mine." Remember, these are their thoughts or utterances about you.

Hone it down until it's in its simplest (and worst) form.

Write the Worst-You statement next to that person's bubble. Be sure it starts with the word *You*.

Checkpoint!

Now look carefully at the Worst-You statement. Is it really the worst? If not, improve on it until you're satisfied it's really the worst thing you can imagine the person saying or thinking about you.

Next, go through the same procedure with the best thought or utterance. What is the best thought or utterance you can imagine this same person thinking or saying about you? Put it in the form of a short statement that starts with You:

"You're really okay, you aren't as bad as everybody says you are, you're very entertaining even if I can't stand to be around you."

For example, Gay recalls a moment from high school: "My mother and I were having an argument. I asked her if she could think of any good qualities about me (she'd been listing off a lot of the other kind). She said to me, 'You're unfettered by convention.' I heard a lot of envy in the background of the statement, a wistfulness that she couldn't be that way, as well as slight disapproval." He would write, "You're unfettered by convention" as his Best-You statement next to her bubble.

Write the Best-You statement next to that person's bubble.

Checkpoint!

Remember, these are your imaginings and memories of their thoughts and opinions. They don't have to make sense, and they may or may not have anything to do with reality.

Next, choose another bubble.

Generate this person's Worst-You/Best-You statements about you. Write a short Worst-You statement and Best-You statement next to that person's bubble. Keep on until you have Worst-You/Best-You statements for all your bubbles.

Step Four: Worst Them, Best Them

Now, turn the tables and do the same thing with your worst and best thoughts about each of the people on your bubble diagram.

Jot down your own simple Worst/Best statements next to one person's bubble.

What is the worst thing you have thought or said about that person? Be as petty, unenlightened, and blunt as you possibly can.

Now, what is the best thing you have thought or said about that person? Be extremely positive, even if you can't imagine saying it to the person's face.

Be brief, simple, and to the point.

For example, the worst thing Gay can recall ever thinking about his mother was, "You didn't ever really love me—it was all made up, something you forced yourself to do." "I'm pretty sure I never said that to her out loud, because picturing it even now I imagine her exploding and going up in smoke. The best thought I can think of is, 'You're a unique combination of love and intelligence.' I'm pretty sure I said that or things like that to her, but I know for sure I've thought it."

Generate a Worst-Them and Best-Them statement for each person, and jot them next to their bubbles.

Step Five

Select a person on your bubble diagram with whom you've had a lot of conflict. It could be a parent or someone else, but make sure it's a person with at least a –2 Energy Rating.

Select the person's Worst-You statement about you.

If you're playing Constellation with a companion, ask that person to role-play the person in the bubble. Ask your companion to say the Worst-You statement to you several times, looking you straight in the eyes. For example, suppose you're working with your Uncle Fred's bubble, and his Worst-You statement is, "You don't belong in this family." Ask your companion to say "You don't belong in this family" to you several times.

If you're playing by yourself, step into the other person's reality for a moment in your imagination. Imagine the person saying it to you several times.

Now, ask yourself: What would be my typical defensive reaction to that statement? If Fred said that to me in an argument, would I argue with it by saying something like, "Yes, I *do* belong in this family!" Or would I do some other kind of defensive move, such as storming out the door? If you're working with a companion, tell the person what your usual defensive move might be.

Okay, time for some distilled wisdom. Do whatever you need to do to get ready to receive some major-league, life-altering enlightenment: prick up your ears, stand on tiptoe, take a deep breath.

Here it comes:

This Worst-You statement you just heard is just a thought and a puff of air. Your companion created a thought, then expressed it with a puff of air. Even if your Uncle Fred actually said it once upon a time, and the entire world agreed with it, it was still just a thought and a puff of air. That's all it was.

Here comes an even bigger life-altering notion: It's our act of getting defensive that locks in the Worst-You statement and makes it real. If we didn't treat it as real and true, we'd have no need to get defensive. Getting defensive is the cue that you're taking something as true and real. For instance, you flinch in a 3-D movie theater when an imaginary spear is hurled at the audience. Your body would have no reason to flinch unless it took the spear as real.

If another person says, "You're stupid" to you, he or she wants you to either get defensive or agree. The other person is trying to get you to say, "No, I'm not!" or "You're absolutely right." (The last one is a remote likelihood—when's the last time you said, "You know . . . you're absolutely right," when another person was attacking you?) If you do either one—agree or get defensive—the thought gets locked in as a reality.

There's an entirely different alternative.

What if you did neither?

What if you didn't agree and you didn't get defensive?

Imagine doing something very different with the Worst-You statement . . . something brand new.

Imagine reacting nondefensively. Imagine reacting to it as what it is—just a thought or a puff of air.

What would that look and sound like?

Here are three examples of nondefensive responses to someone saying, "You don't belong in this family":

1. "Hmm—that's an interesting thought. I wonder if there's anything valuable I could learn from it?"

2. "Hmm—I've had that thought myself from time to time, but I've never really let myself consider it fully."

3. "Thank you. I feel angry (or scared or sad) when I hear you say that, and I feel the urge to defend myself. Instead, I'm going to take a deep breath." (Breathe in . . . breathe out.)

Keep those ears pricked . . . we're not quite finished yet.

Why aren't nondefended reactions more popular, and why is defensiveness so popular? Why do many people have the same argument over and over for years without any resolution?

Here's why: Usually, we're afraid to drop our defensive reaction because we think that if we don't defend ourselves the other person's idea will become real. The person says, "You're stupid." If we didn't defend ourselves—"No I'm not!"—the idea that we're stupid would become reality.

Let's hear that again: We think we have to defend ourselves to keep the other person's thoughts from becoming real.

That's upside down from how it actually works. The act of defending ourselves is based on assuming the other person's version is real. If you didn't think it was real, you wouldn't feel any urge to defend yourself.

It's *our* defensive move that makes *their* thought real. The other person realizes this unconsciously as soon as you get defensive. Your defensiveness sends a signal to the other person that he or she is on the right track. They've got you rattled. Then the other person usually sniffs victory and turns up the volume on the attack.

But there's something even more important we all need to know.

The very best reason to drop defensiveness is that each time we lock in on a position (such as defending ourselves against a thought or utterance like "You're stupid") we clinch around it—and this clinch stops the flow of connection. Crazy as it may sound, the other person probably wouldn't say "You're stupid" unless he or she had some kind of love and caring for you.

The other person—that annoying entity who's telling you

"You're stupid"—is usually trying to express some sort of love for you, and that's the best way he or she knows how.

That may sound nutty, but isn't it true? Picture yourself saying something critical to another person you care about.

GAY: I'm picturing myself saying to my mother, which I did a bunch of times, always without success, "Stop smoking! It's stupid! Those things are going to kill you!" In fact, they eventually did. Whenever I mounted one of my Quit Smoking offensives against her, she got defensive. I never learned, and she never did, either. This whole melodrama was the best way we knew how to express our love for each other. I wish we'd figured out a better way, but I also wish the bin men came on Monday and Wednesday like the schedule says. They don't, no matter how many times we call.

When people play the Constellation game in our seminars, they invariably discover two happy surprises at the end of the process. First, they discover that the Worst-You thoughts disappear into thin air after they're discussed, while the Best-You thoughts remain in the form of pleasant after-sensations. Second, and perhaps most important, is the discovery that the situations that in the past triggered defensiveness and other unpleasant reactions are now "no big deal." The act of playing Constellation takes the sting out of the past, replacing it with an easy sense of acceptance.

Issue 6:

Clarity

What is Clarity?

Clarity is a communication tool that increases creativity, productivity, and ease in close relationships. It does so by reducing communication breakdowns and relationship strains. With Clarity, you can expect a significant speedup in project completions.

It can also be used in the business world; companies that use Clarity long term (from six to twelve months) significantly reduce sick days, absenteeism, and insurance utilization, while building morale and job satisfaction.

Clarity is implemented at first with a worksheet; however, once you incorporate Clarity into your way of thinking, you will seldom need to use the worksheet.

How does Clarity work?

Communication breakdowns and relationship strains always involve at least one of the following events:

1. People make unclear agreements, resulting in a lack of clarity on what's been agreed to.

2. People break agreements. After agreements are broken, there is lack of clarity about how to repair the damage.

3. People do not speak about significant feelings and/or facts.

4. People blame each other when problems are encountered, focusing on who's to blame rather than what needs to get done.

Here's an example Breakdown Scenario: Ed, a manager, talks to Mary and John about elements of a proposal that he wants on his desk by 5 p.m. The meeting ends with a hazy agreement: Ed thinks they've agreed to deliver something specific by 5, Mary thinks that delivering at 5 is a noble goal but doesn't hear it as an agreement, and John thinks delivering at 5 is totally unrealistic but doesn't say so. At 5:10, Ed calls them and asks where it is. A flurry of excuses ensues: John says he's waiting for some input from Mary so he can finish his part. Mary says John was supposed to ask Waldo to get some input to her but John didn't get hold of Waldo yet. Ed gets angry and blames John and Mary. They get defensive, make more excuses, and point more blame back and forth. They're also feeling hurt and angry but hide their feelings because they're afraid Ed will blow up even more.

Clarity eliminates that scenario in thirty seconds of preventive maintenance and a template for rapid resolution if breakdown occurs. With Clarity, the emphasis is never on blame but on learning what needs to be learned and doing what needs to be done.

The Breakdown Scenario

A hazy agreement is made OR a significant fact or feeling is withheld. ⟶ An agreement is broken. ⟶ Blame is directed at others or self (What's wrong with you? What's wrong with me? What's wrong with them?). ➝ Defensiveness and excuses abound. ➝ People entrench and justify their positions. ➝ Withdrawal and loss of trust ensue. ➝ Discouragement, or worse—illness, sabotage, revenge—rear up.

The Clarity Scenario

A clear agreement is made. ➝ Significant facts and feelings are aired. ➝ Completion occurs.

Or if not:

Breakdown is reviewed quickly with no blame, clear communication of feelings and facts, identification of what each person learned from the situation, and recommitment to a new agreement or to renew the old agreement.

The Clarity Worksheet

Use the following form when you implement Clarity. If you do not succeed at first, simply fill out the form and try again.

1. We agree that _____

_____

(action agreement) will happen by/at_____

_____

_____ (time agreement).

2. _____

takes responsibility for certifying completion.

3. We agree to make any change in the agreement by direct communication, mutually agreed upon.

4. Initialed and agreed to by _____

_____

Fact/Feeling Check

I make it safe for me and others to speak freely about any feelings and facts.

As I make this agreement I'm aware of:

____ Anxiety, fear, nervousness

____ Irritation, anger, aggravation, resentment

____ Discouragement, sadness, resignation

____ Excitement, happiness, exhilaration

____ Other feelings

____ Significant facts

_____

_____

_____

_____

If failure occurs, we agree to review the reasons and identify our learning edge, doing our best to take 100 percent responsibility and avoid blame.

Reason Check

____ I failed to estimate accurately the time/resources necessary to complete.

____ I failed to communicate relevant facts and/or feelings.

___ I made the agreement with no intention of keeping it.

___ I made the agreement to please _____.

___ I made the agreement to get _____ off my back.

___ I forgot we had an agreement.

___ I "couldn't" do it because _____

_____.

___ I was afraid to say "No" at the time because _____

_____.

___ I changed my mind and failed to tell you.

___ I didn't realize you were serious.

___ You "made" me agree to it and I hid my feelings about that.

___ Not keeping agreements is one of my patterns of self-sabotage.

___ Not speaking relevant facts and feelings is one of my patterns of self-sabotage.

___ Other (please list)

_____

_____

_____

_____

Issue 7:

How to Eliminate Jealousy

The first important thing to know about jealousy is that it doesn't exist. Jealousy is impossible to deal with in close relationships because it's not real. In helping hundreds of people eliminate jealousy, we've never seen anybody get rid of it by approaching it on the level of "jealousy."

The Only Way

The only way to handle jealousy in the real world of relationships is to shift your state of consciousness so that you can see jealousy for what it really is beneath the surface. The dictionary tells us that jealousy is when you're "fearful of losing affection or being supplanted by another person." It also says we're jealous when we're "vigilant in guarding something." These are helpful pointers to the real issues underneath jealousy.

Jealousy Is Really about Fear and Control

When you're jealous you're scared. Fear is real—you can feel its racy-queasy butterflies in your belly. You're afraid of losing the love of the other person. We often magnify our fear, though, by expressing it in the distorted form of anger. If we could say to the other person, "I'm scared I'm losing your love," we could move through the mire of the situation much more quickly. Instead of confronting our fears directly, we often get angry and blame the other person. This keeps us from focusing inwardly to find out what we're really scared about.

When you're jealous you're also trying to control the other person and his or her feelings. Here's where many of us have gotten into very sticky relationship dramas. Gay recalls the painful experience of getting dumped at nineteen by his girlfriend, Alice:

GAY: I'd been in love with her since we were at high school. I think from the moment I met her I assumed we'd always be together. Then, in our second year of college, she fell in love with another boy. I went through many levels of anger before I was finally able to confront my real fears and grief. First, I angrily tried to talk her out of it by listing all the faults and flaws of the guy she was dumping me for. I made up lies about him and hurled them at her. When that didn't work I tried guilt: How could you betray everything we've gone through together? Nothing worked! The harder I tried to hang on to her the more I saw the love in her eyes turn to pity.

The reason control never works is that we're trying to control something that's uncontrollable. Whether another person loves us is fundamentally out of our control. Remember Epictetus, who made this point clearly in the opening line of his *Art of Living:* The secret of happiness is knowing that "some things are within our control, and some things are not." The reason jealousy makes us so miserable is that we expend our energy trying to control the other person rather than turning that energy inward to explore our real feelings.

Eliminating Jealousy
Is a Two-Step Process

First, you have to find out what you're really afraid of. Usually, it's a fear of abandonment, of being alone, of not feeling whole and sufficient on your own. There's often grief as well as fear buried beneath the jealousy. We've often never fully recovered from some earlier abandonment or betrayal, and the open wound of this old trauma drives our desperate attempt to control the other person in our present.

The second step is to talk about the fear and grief openly, preferably with the person you're jealous about. If this isn't possible, a friend, coach, or therapist can sometimes step in to provide the support and listening ear we all need at such times.

What's Possible in a
Conscious Relationship

In a healthy, conscious relationship, jealousy doesn't recycle because the partners talk about it on a deeper level. They talk about their fears, their old griefs, and what they want and need from the other person in the present. If you get underneath the anger and control of jealousy to the real feelings of fear and grief, you'll find that the jealousy dissolves naturally and doesn't return.

Issue 8:

How to Grow a Conscious Relationship

Almost every day we get requests from people seeking permission to use the words from our poster, *HOW TO GROW A CONSCIOUS RELATIONSHIP*. Most often, the requests are from people who want to use them as part of their wedding vows. The words themselves were first written by Gay in the 1980s. Thanks to the beautiful graphics by Fran Sloan and Tracey Ryder, the poster has gone on to grace thousands of walls around the world. You may view the new version of the poster at www.hendricks.com.

Herewith are our best teachings, in their most distilled form, for you to use at weddings and other celebratory events. May you be as inspired by the ideas as we have been, and may all your relationships grow as magnificently as ours has by putting the ideas into practice.

How to Grow a Conscious Relationship

First, love yourself deeply. . . . Genuine love for *you* attracts genuine love from others.

Ask yourself three questions:

Is a conscious relationship something I really want?

Am I willing to commit to one person with all my heart?

Am I willing to do whatever work it takes on myself to enjoy Lasting Love?

Tune in deeply to your needs. . . .

Find out what you really want in a close relationship.

Remember: The past is past. . . . It doesn't need to color your present and your future.

BREATHE! BREATHE! BREATHE! Breathe in love for yourself . . . breathe out love for everyone around you.

Feel all your feelings . . . and give everyone around you room to feel all their feelings.

Keep your promises impeccably: Do what you say you'll do . . . and don't do what you say you won't do.

Appreciate yourself and your loved ones out loud at least once an hour.

Treat yourself to lots of alone time . . . and give the gift of solitude to others around you when they need it.

Tell the truth all ways and always.

CELEBRATE YOURSELF for having created the life you're living, and CELEBRATE YOURSELF for being willing to change it.

Breath and love are sure cures for fear. . . . Love all your fears and breathe through them to more love.

Love as much as you can from wherever you are at the moment.

Tune in often to your deepest self: Am I honoring my true essence—who I truly am? Am I honoring the essence of those around me?

Remember: A beautiful garden grows one day at a time—careful nurturing honors the gift of nature and celebrates it.

Index

Underlined page references indicate boxed text.

M

N

OTHER RODALE BOOKS
AVAILABLE FROM PAN MACMILLAN

1-4050-2100-4	The Anorexia Diaries	*Tara Rio and Linda Rio*	£8.99
1-4050-4182-X	The Doctors' Book of Home Remedies	*A Prevention Health Book*	£20.00
1-4050-6718-7	Healing Without Freud or Prozac	*Dr David Servan-Schreiber*	£12.99
1-4050-3339-8	The Immune Advantage	*Ellen Mazo*	£14.99
1-4050-0671-4	Laying Down the Law	*Dr Ruth Peters*	£8.99
1-4050-4103-X	The New Brain	*Dr Richard Restak*	£10.99
1-4050-0675-7	The Secret Life of the Dyslexic Child	*Robert Frank with Kathryn Livingston*	£10.99
1-4050-3340-1	When Your Body Gets the Blues	*Marie-Annette Brown and Jo Robinson*	£10.99

All Pan Macmillan titles can be ordered from our website, *www.panmacmillan.com*, or from your local bookshop and are also available by post from:

Bookpost, PO Box 29, Douglas, Isle of Man IM99 1BQ
Tel: 01624 836000; fax: 01624 670923; e-mail: *bookshop@enterprise.net*;
or visit: *www.bookpost.co.uk*. Credit cards accepted. Free postage and packing in the United Kingdom

Prices shown above were correct at time of going to press.
Pan Macmillan reserve the right to show new retail prices on covers which may differ from those previously advertised in the text or elsewhere.

For information about buying *Rodale* titles in **Australia**, contact Pan Macmillan Australia. Tel: 1300 135 113; fax: 1300 135 103;
e-mail: *customer.service@macmillan.com.au*; or visit: *www.panmacmillan.com.au*

For information about buying *Rodale* titles in **New Zealand**, contact Macmillan Publishers New Zealand Limited. Tel: (09) 414 0356; fax: (09) 414 0352;
e-mail: *lyn@macmillan.co.nz*; or visit: *www.macmillan.co.nz*

For information about buying *Rodale* titles in **South Africa**, contact Pan Macmillan South Africa. Tel: (011) 325 5220; fax: (011) 325 5225;
e-mail: *roshni@panmacmillan.co.za*